Bachelor*ista

ISBN: 978-0615783253

The Bachelorista Giving Tree

Living in the heart of all Bacheloristas is the desire to make the world a better place. That's why 10 percent of the profits from this book—and all we do—go directly to charity. To learn more about the organizations we support, visit us at www.Bachelorista.com.

The Life & Luck of a Bachelorista

A Valentine to Single Women

By Monica Bossinger

Dear Bachelorista,

You have so much to be grateful for. We're living in a society filled with endless possibilities for single women. This evening, Anderson Cooper interviewed a North Dakota woman who married herself. Although most of us don't have that particular desire, I give the lady props for single-handedly taking herself off the market—only in America. Belles, you don't have to marry yourself to find purpose in your life. But if you feel the need, I know a great florist.

I hope you find empowerment, solidarity, encouragement, and a bit of humor in the following pages.

We're better together,

Monica

CONTENTS

ACKNOWLEDGMENTS

A resounding thank you to Laura Chekow, Mara Clearspring, Traci Mosser, Jennifer D. Duff, Isabelle Fregevu-Claracq, Nancy Moy, Sherri Lerner, and my brother Werner for making this book a wonderful adventure.

Bachelorista - bach·e·lor·ista
– A savvy woman who blazes through her single years like a rock star, radiating gratitude for her life.

PREFACE

More than a dozen years ago, I had a tarot card reading. According to my fortune-teller, the road ahead looked rosy. But when she turned my love card over, we took an unpleasant detour. The image revealed a man bound by rope, head-to-toe against a tree. Hmm. Tortured? Clearly it wasn't the prediction I expected, but the caution that followed, "You'll learn to be very independent," made me laugh. I've always been a free spirit, and on many levels, I believe we choose our own destinies.

But it did make me wonder. What would my life look like if I never married, had kids, or grew old with someone? In the midst of my trying to figure it all out in a way that worked for me, the question of my marital status often came up in conversation. Like millions of single women, I heard my share of "Why are you still single?" The best unapologetic response I've heard to this is, "Just lucky, I guess."

The single man has it easier. Whether he's a twenty-something golden boy or an aging artist, he's not worried about his marital status, he's just doing his thing. While guys don't wrestle with the challenges of a biological clock, there's something to be said for his nonchalance. The most important part being that he's enjoying his single life and not wishing it away.

While America has made some strides in supporting single women in the last few decades, in deep pockets of our society there's still a double standard when it comes to marriage. On the one hand, a good old boy is slapping his son on the back saying, "Take it from me: Don't rush into marriage." But then the same guy looks at a single woman over 35 as if she had two heads. And in fairness, it's not just the old guard passing judgment. For me, the "Why hasn't someone snatched you up by now?" question came from every direction. Acting as if they wanted to understand my disease, curious strangers, people at work and men I dated said things like, "Maybe you're too picky" and "What's the longest relationship you've ever had?"

None of this is news. We're living in a numbers and labels society that says if you're over a certain age and never married, then you've got deep-seated flaws that make you unmarriable. Well, it seems the clerks at town hall forgot to send me the memo that said they'd only grant marriage licenses to unflawed people with extraordinary partnership skills. If the institution had no casualties because all the participants were perfect (and perfectly happy), then perhaps being single would say something meaningful about an individual's character. I guess the bigger question is why society cares whether we're married or not. Pressuring singles to fit into a box that only works for 50 percent of married people is crazy talk.

I'm not down on the institution. In fact, for a long time, I wanted to be married in a big way. I wish I could say that I behaved like one of those cool people above the desire to tie the knot—like the fabulous Diane Keaton. In my 20s, I met a few women with her laid-back attitude toward marriage. They acted like they didn't care, and men ate it up. Indifference seemed sexy to me, but at the time I didn't know how to be that unaffected. Regular sex mingled with emotional and financial security? Hell, yes! Sign me up. The process of letting go of the life I thought I wanted took more years than I'd like to admit.

When it came to love, I made many missteps because I didn't want to be *that* girl. You know, the adult at the kids' table, the coworker arriving solo to the Christmas party, the 45-year-old bridesmaid in the lavender dress. I tried to make things work with the wrong people. I can tell you with certainty that the shortcuts I took on the path to finding happiness were antithetical to success. Years ago, I wasted precious time in a tumultuous relationship with an alcoholic. We went to high school together and I don't remember a time that I wasn't smitten by his Robert Redford looks and charm. Looking back, I should have dropped him after our second date, but my desire for a "plus one" (and for Robert Redford!) made me feel as powerless as my friend felt about his disease.

Before truly healthy relationships arrived, I had some inner work to do. My breakthrough came on the other side of that self-improvement tunnel, when my marital status became irrelevant to me. I felt happy and free for the first time in my life. As for you, Bachelorista, if there's only one thing that you take away from this book, I hope it's this: There's no reason why your single years can't be the happiest ones of your life.

Whether we're empowered and cruising through singlehood happily or crashing on the path of resistance, we are the architects of our destiny. The more we take responsibility for our happiness, the more fun life becomes. Besides, there's nothing sexy about bitterness and blaming others for the compromises we make. We're too smart for that.

My love life looks very different today. I've channeled my inner Diane Keaton, and I don't feel the need to try anymore. In fact, I don't try at all. It feels a-w-e-s-o-m-e. I no longer think that the pasture is greener over there in Marriage Land. I live, unapologetic, in a sweet little hamlet called Bacheloristaville, and I have everything I need. When I reflect on the decades I've been single (yes, it's been that long), I feel grateful for the lessons these years have taught me, painful as some of them were. But as a student of life and love, I now consider myself lucky for each and every debacle. They were all seeds of better things to come.

I try not to think about the time that I've wasted hoping for the dream guy, kids, white picket fence and robust 401k. Today, I have my navigation set to unadulterated fun, empowerment, gratitude, spirituality, and self-love. I finally know where I'm going. Halle-f--king-lujah.

When I stopped trying to make my life fit into a traditional mold, I felt alive in a way that I hadn't in years. But why stop there? I want to enjoy the pulp out of life. I want to devour the things I love. And more than anything, I want to take every crazy-stupid limiting belief I've ever heard outside. I want to kick it up and down a gritty New York City street and then bury it deep into the earth away from the vampires who feed on it. Thankfully, I don't give a flying f--k about conventional 'wisdom' anymore. I used to live in that world. I've cried my tears. I've survived that hell. And since channeling the laws of retribution, I've left it behind for heavenly things. And now I can't stop laughing.

For Meghan Shea, Emma Rose, Mia Sara, and
Bacheloristas everywhere.

THE LIFE AND LUCK OF A BACHELORISTA

PIPPI
PATRON ANGEL OF BACHELORISTAS

Before we begin, I'd like to introduce Pippi, the Patron Angel of Bacheloristas and my spiritual sidekick. Unpredictable, playful and all heart, Pippi pipes up here and there to share her thoughts with you. In her own special way, she's on a mission to empower Bacheloristas around the globe. As you can imagine, Pippi's busy.

THE LIFE AND LUCK OF A BACHELORISTA

"Do not spoil what you have by desiring what you have not; remember that what you now have was once among the things you only hoped for."

– Epicurus

CHAPTER 1

LUCK LOVES THIS LADY

Dear Bachelorista,

Last night, I dreamt that I married a man in my past. From the Cracker Jack ring he gave me to the honeymoon we spent with my family to the tiny apartment we lived in, every part of our life together felt wrong. To make matters worse, his family made a cameo and I sat in a living room across from his gangsta sister—a woman I once knew. When I awoke, I couldn't shake off the dream. It felt so real that it haunted me all day. What made this nightmare worse than my usual variety—the ones where bad guys are chasing me—is that it could have actually happened.

The next time we lament our single status, let's try to remember how lucky we are. Without in-laws, marital strife, difficult children, minivans, and diaper runs, our lives are pretty damn good. Maggie, it's time to take stock of our good fortune.

Love this moment,

Monica

Bachelorista takeaway: You're blooming
Marrying a man for the wrong reasons is like hoping the wrinkle cream will work. You're going to wake up 20 years from now and realize you've spent your youth—and rosy complexion—on a lie.

Pippi pipes up: If you're in the habit of expecting miracles like summer snow and flying puppies, then become a fiction writer, and make it work for you. Someone's going to be the next J.K. Rowling; it may as well be you.

Bachelorista takeaway: You've got that special thing
Lovely, if the voice within us wants what is best—self-preservation, peace, happiness, and to lead us to our higher purpose, why do we ignore it? One way we search outside ourselves for answers is by reading books about how to land a guy. How many single men do you know who study the nuances of female commitment in their free time? None! They are living their lives, taking over the world, and having fun. What the f--k are we doing Ladybug? Let's stop squeezing our awesomeness into a magazine-calibrated pretzel pose. Show up as you are. It's plenty enough, I promise. If he doesn't see how fabulous you are, he's not your man. Besides, that whole contorted pose thingy is not only unbecoming, it's a diversion. Instead of hanging out and waiting for him to call, you could use that time to run for office, invent something useful, laugh with your friends, or make the world a better place.

When I was young and untrusting, I heard that instinctive voice but often ignored it. One hundred percent of the time, I'd regret it. Let's always place our bets on our inner knowing. We're fortunate to have a finely tuned intuitive guide working on our behalf.

Bachelorista takeaway: You're skipping this rodeo
Once you're on the marriage track, people are pushy. Friends

and family pressure married couples into having children all the time. I know Bacheloristas are strong-armed too–especially when it comes to settling down–but you don't have to worry about your partner caving in, or worse–siding with his mother.

Bachelorista takeaway: No stranger danger here

Today, single people have more opportunities than ever to meet interesting people. With no hubby buffer, we're more exposed to the world. Recently, I met a cool scientific journalist on a plane ride to Newark. We spent the entire flight talking about global warming, her soon-to-be published book, and what real estate pockets to avoid due to rising sea levels. If I had an old man, he'd be eating peanuts in her seat and I might have invested in a sinking split-level.

I've heard people say that being single leads to selfishness and rigidity. I think it does the opposite. Bacheloristas who are working and engaged in the world are out and about joining conversations, enjoying adventures, traveling, and expanding their beliefs. In other words, we're busy becoming open-minded people. Lila, we lead charmed lives.

Bachelorista takeaway: It's always our station

Ever wonder what the soundtrack of your life would be like? I can't recall a period in mine without remembering an artist or song that went with it–whether swinging my pigtails to "The Candy Man" from *Willy Wonka:*

"Who can take a sunrise
Sprinkle it in dew
Cover it in chocolate
and a miracle or two?
The candyman.
The candyman can
The candyman can cause he mixes it with love and
makes the world taste good."

Or tuning into the Beatles the day I got braces or blowing out speakers to "Free Falling" in college. Music is powerful. And so is the fact that I don't have to listen to his Nine Inch Nails CD bouncing off the walls of my apartment. Bacheloristas, how lucky are we?

Pippi pipes up: I blast harp music.

Bachelorista takeaway: The stakes are high when marrieds say buh-bye

If a marriage ends and a woman has children, she'll have to explain to them why daddy lives somewhere else. And worse, she may have to see her ex (and possibly his new partner) during every milestone of her children's lives. Luckily for us, if it's quitting time, we can say "fini" and walk away forever.

Bachelorista takeaway: It's fun in the sandbox

Remember when you were young and you loved playing in the sandbox? Anyone could jump in and crash the party. Singlehood is an adventure like that. You get to swing your flowered bucket around next to anyone you choose.

In my fifth year, my family and I lived in an adorable red-shuttered white cape in East Meadow, New York. One gloomy spring afternoon, after yet another solid day of rain, I looked out from the den window into our backyard. The sky had cleared. Straight below, I spied something out-of-this-world awesome: four square feet of frothy mud. I remember thinking that nature gifted me that mud puddle—"Sorry for the days confined indoors, little lady, have at it." I asked my mother if I could go outside and play in the mud. It's the first time in my life that I remember wanting something so bad that I couldn't see past it. I must have equated that mud puddle with something gigantic because when she said that I wasn't allowed to get dirty in that way, her words hit me like a hurricane. That brownie-sundae pool of fun invited me to play. It called ME! She didn't understand. I tried everything to change her mind: "I'll put on my rain boots and jacket." She wouldn't budge. Finally, at the top of my lungs, I screamed, "I want to be a pig!" I needed to hurt her back in the same piercing way she hurt me. This meant war. For a year or two following this, I wrote my mother hate mail. I knew my behavior wasn't ladylike or kind, but it didn't stop me from penning variations of "You are a pig." It took my pint-sized heart a long time to forgive her. Because my mom is a kind, gracious woman, and not in the habit of denying any of us fun, I still feel a little twinge of shame for going rogue. I have no idea if she remembers my rudimentary scribbling. But I have and always will go out of my way to joyfully stomp through mud puddles.

Pippi pipes up: Bachelorista, I hope you give the child inside permission to come out and play.

Bachelorista takeaway: Bon voyage, sucker

When you're single, you can book your vacations spontaneously. Ireland in September, Venice in spring—you decide. Most Americans get a few measly weeks of vacation each year. Lucky Bacheloristas can spend those precious days exactly as they wish.

In 2000, my single friend Liz moved abroad. She found an apartment near the Vatican and spent a few lovely years living in Rome. When I went to visit, I had a ten-day window into her fabulous, anything-is-possible life. And then she sent me packing.

Bachelorista takeaway: It's not easy on Trishna

Not every woman gets to choose her own destiny. There are still cultures today where arranged marriages are the norm. Luckily, we're living in a country that allows us to choose our partners.

Pippi pipes up: True that.

Bachelorista takeaway: We're staying

Can't imagine leaving the cute New England enclave you call home? Or the West Village apartment you never dreamed you'd find? Well Lady Love, you don't have to. But somewhere right now a missus is losing a wager, and moving 5,000 miles from family and friends.

My mother did the transatlantic move with five kids in tow so we could be near my dad's family in Germany. A crazy amount of cuckoo clocks later, we hightailed it back to New York with a trunk full of Bavarian pretzels and lederhosen. Auf Wiedersehen, Oma.

Bachelorista takeaway: We can adopt little rascals

We don't need a man to adopt a baby and name him Spanky. Luckily, singles have fewer obstacles today if they choose parenthood. While there are many benefits to two-parent homes, why should single women with love to give forfeit their dreams of motherhood because they're unattached? Life is complicated. Love is complicated. I think women are adapting beautifully. **Pippi pipes up: You're the only one who gets to decide what family means to you.**

Bachelorista takeaway: Crash the party

If someone fun has the Taylor Swift-like courage to crash a ho-ity-toity party you're at, take it upon yourself to thank her. You and I know it's probably a bloody bore. Dull people don't crash parties. They're home watching *Wheel of Fortune* practicing the alphabet. Give me a "Y" give me an "A" give me a "W," give me an "N."

Bachelorista takeaway: Decisions by committee are a crapshoot

As a Bachelorista, you get to decide what you bring into your life. As opposed to compromising on say…just about everything.

Sally: "Babe, look, this kitten is so adorable. She's purring at me. I think this is the one."
Rick: "I'd rather go with the potbelly."

When my married friend Preston decided to buy a new car last year, he chose a practical model completely within the realm of affordability. But his wife wanted him to get a less expensive car. Preston is tall and he didn't quite fit into the smaller sedan she chose. But since he just wanted to keep the peace, he bought the car she preferred. After a month, he brought it back to the dealership. When he learned how much money he would lose by trading it in for the original car he wanted, he settled on his existing wheels. When I asked him about it, he said "Everything's decided by committee in our home." Holy moly, I wish this story wasn't true. No one strong-arms a Bachelorista into purchasing something she doesn't want.

Bachelorista takeaway: 'Bom chicka wah wah' is here to stay
When you're single, flirting isn't a crime.
Hubby: "I saw you looking at him."
Wife: "At who?"
Hubby: "The waiter."
Wife: "I just gave him my order."
Hubby: "You were making eyes at him."
Wife: "Oh, you mean the way my pupils dilated when he said I'll get jasmine rice with the salmon?"
Pippi pipes up: Fortunately, Bacheloristas can flirt wherever, whenever they choose. Hoo-ha.

Bachelorista takeaway: It's hard for Mrs. Himster to dodge his dogs
You don't need to hide your disdain for his buddies, mother or sister over the long haul. If you're dating and his entourage drives you nuts, you can wiggle out of invitations. Or dump him. When you're married, you're kind of stuck, possibly forever.

Bachelorista takeaway: "Uncomplicated" helps me sleep at night
When you're single and the phone rings, the day can take you anywhere. You don't need to argue with your husband about the fact that you've gone out three times this week or worry that your toddler's meltdowns are because you're not with him enough.

One summer, years ago, my friend Jane called. After a "Let's do dinner at Xichos" discussion, we invited another friend along and the three of us dined al fresco at a downtown Mexican restaurant. We sat under the stars eating Shitake Chipotle and Mole Poblano while working on our sangrias. I felt antsy that night and asked the ladies if they could remember the last time they did something memorable. Long story short, we paid the bill and then crashed a rock concert in the next town—it didn't cost us anything and we managed to get great seats. The conversation (and the night) might have gone differently if one of us were married. Being free makes evenings like this possible.

Bachelorista takeaway: Kids are like a mirror
My married sister, Susan, is 13 months older than I am. In my mind, there's a decade between us and I'm a change-of-life baby. It has nothing to do with her. The fact that I'm not the mother of two teenagers makes me feel much younger than my age. Without children growing up before my eyes, I don't have a constant reminder of where I'm at chronologically. When it does hit me, I cover all the mirrors in my apartment until I feel 30 again. **Pippi pipes up: Without the huge responsibilities of marriage and parenting, you can live like a rock star.**

Bachelorista takeaway: No Saturday nights with the in-laws
Live your single life like it's your last day alone. If you have a family, you'll need to put your loved ones' needs before your own. Honeybuns, that means seizing the moment and living it up while you can.

When my sister Nina was alive, she made the weekly one-hour drive to her husband Charlie's parents' home for dinner every Saturday night for 23 years. She loved Charlie's family but hoped that after their son arrived, these family dinners would become less frequent (I'm thinking harvest moons). Because she loved him and Charlie made sacrifices for her, Nina continued to go with him.

If you intend to marry someday, you can bet on the fact that your partner will ask you to do the exact opposite of what you feel like doing sometimes.

Bachelorista takeaway: Someone is chasing down a wild child
Parenthood is risky business. There's no guarantee that your children will become decent human beings. In my family, a few of my siblings handled growing up in our crazy-strict household better than others. Like a child drafted into the military, I wasn't cut out for all the rules. From the sports I had to play to the daily rosary to our health-food only diets to our Saturday morning cleaning marathons to our early bedtime—every inch of our lives was compartmentalized and patrolled. My father also had rules against crying, getting sick, and swearing. By the time I turned 10, it dawned on me that there would be many more years with the "General." So when my parents weren't looking, I, in a very unladylike fashion, went ape shit.

First, I began hanging around Kiki, the only true badass in the sixth grade. She initiated me to the fine art of smoking marijuana, streaking, and lifting knickknacks without attracting attention. After introducing Kiki to my parents, my adventures with her came to an immediate end. By the age of 12, I hit the height of my rebellion. My friend Amy and I babysat for a couple in our town. We put the kiddos to bed, invited some boys over, blasted Fleetwood Mac, and got blitzed. We hid the evidence in true tween style by rolling a dozen beer bottles under the sofa and throwing the couple's empty vodka bottles in their backyard. By the time high school came around, besides throwing wild parties with my siblings when my parents left town, I felt tame in comparison to my classmates.

Moonshine, if you were a rebel, your children may be even crazier than you were. Before that thought settles in, ask yourself if you've played all your wild cards. If not, you're going to want to do that before baby Lottie arrives.

Pippi pipes up: Worrying about firecracker kids can take years off your life. You're spared, Principessa.

PIPPI'S POW-WOW
Save the Date!

Ready to throw a party, Bachelorista? I'll take your silence as a "Yes." If you're up for it, this is fun. Where to begin? Choose a night when you and your friends are free. You're going to invite Bachelors and Bacheloristas to your place for a "bring your own single story" (BYOSS) party. You'll need to buy one gift prize—something along the lines of a bottle of wine, movie tickets, or a gift certificate to a local restaurant. If you're short on cash, pool the money with your friends or make it a BYOB.

On the e-vite, ask your guests to arrive with a typed dating story—an account of something wacky, funny, or just interesting that happened to them (a paragraph will do)—and let them know the story must be anonymous. When the guests arrive (you look fabulous by the way), put their dating stories in a hat. When everyone's had time to mingle, gather your guests and read the first story aloud. The group has three guesses to figure out who wrote the story. Whether the guesses are correct or not, the person who wrote the story gets up and reads the next dating tale. That process continues until all the stories are read aloud. Afterward, ask for an anonymous vote of everyone's favorite anecdote by placing that person's name on a piece of paper (name tags might come in handy here). The host tallies the votes and announces the winner.

Now that the icebreaker part of your evening's over, Bachelorista, I bet you've learned some useful insights about your party guests—including how they view the opposite sex by the stories they chose to share. Good luck mingling with the cool people.

LUCK LOVES THIS LADY

"People often remark that I'm pretty lucky. Luck is only important in so far as getting the chance to sell yourself at the right moment. After that, you've got to have talent and know how to use it."

– Frank Sinatra

CHAPTER 2

WRINKLED PAJAMAS

Dear Bachelorista,

Remember when you were little and wanted nothing more than to be surrounded by your favorite things? You brought your tutu to school, slept with your favorite doll and spent hours pouring imaginary tea into pink plastic cups. You weren't just inspired by these things. They stimulated your imagination, and gave you comfort. We may have aged a few decades, but some things don't change. Creature comforts and nesting are part of our DNA.

This morning I woke up late, the kind of hour you only admit to your single friends. Most of the married people I know don't like to be reminded of lazy mornings sleeping in, then lounging around the house in wrinkled pajamas. On these guilt-free days, it doesn't take long to realize that life is good.

So whether you're kicking back with friends in your bright white beach cottage, hitting your law books in a Soho loft, or painting a masterpiece in a Montana cabin, relish it.

Holding down the fort,

Monica

Bachelorista takeaway: We live on Easy Street

There's an Easy Street in every town. And it's the one you live on if you happen to be single. Unlike Mrs. Commitment, who has to discuss where and how to set up house with her other half, Bacheloristas do as they wish. Kit Cat, hang your blue striped curtains with abandon.

Pippi pipes up: No one puts a lid on the kid.

Bachelorista takeaway: Someone's dragging herself out of bed

Nursing babies, snoring men, failed attempts to have sex, teenagers staying out past curfew—how in the world do married people sleep? Bachelorista, while your pillow-creased face is still on the market, enjoy your REM sleep.

Pippi pipes up: You can sleepwalk and no one has to know—even you. When you make it back to bed and wake up the next morning, the blankets are on your side of the bed.

Bachelorista takeaway: Mrs. Daisy is a constant gardener

Whether the hard work of marriage yields a beautiful arrangement or a mob of weeds, the care and feeding of a partnership is challenging. Chemistry, support and appreciation are not easy to maintain over the long haul—especially given the demands of daily life. Sustaining a romantic relationship in the world seems Herculean today. Half the time (and despite a great deal of work), it simply comes unglued.

Pippi pipes up: Partnership is either a thriving enterprise or a decomposing business. Between these two extremes is the most deceiving of all: mediocrity.

Bachelorista takeaway: You could live in an amusement park

You marry your college boyfriend and you expect that he'll outgrow his hashish-and-SunnyD-for-breakfast stage. But what if he doesn't? With a skate park in your backyard, a scooter in the hall, and a barn full of fireworks, you may be reliving his child-hood dreams until you're 70.

In my 30s, I lived in Maui for a year. I dated a handsome 37-year-old surfer who often used a skateboard to go from point A to point B (I never knew his exact whereabouts). If memory serves, he ended it because I kept forgetting to cut the crust off his peanut butter and jelly sandwiches. Silly me.

Bachelorista takeaway: You could be coerced into parting with Kellogg
I recently read a pet adoption ad at a Berkshire animal shelter that stated a woman was giving up her dog because her fiancé doesn't like animals. I wanted to track her down and discuss her disturbing decision but I figured her intended would clock me before I made it to the front door.

Jay, a NYC man I dated years ago asked me to move in with him. But since his fancy pants dog didn't get along with my cat, Peanut Butter, he suggested that I give him up. Leave my be-loved pet baby? Are you loco? He felt offended that I wouldn't sacrifice my cat in exchange for his love and a Central Park West apartment. Even after I broke it down for puppy breath, "It would be like forfeiting my arm," he still didn't get it.

Bachelorista takeaway: Your wish is your command
We can dance around the house at whim, paint our rooms the color of Jane Iredale eye shadows, and use banana peels as a doormat. It's our prerogative. When I can't sleep, I like rear-ranging furniture. It's not unusual to see my couch inching to-ward the south wall of my living room at 3 a.m. Whenever the inspiration hits, I have the luxury of getting up or winding down, without disturbing anyone.
Pippi pipes up: No one has the potential to live outside the box easier than single people. So tap that toolbox Buttercup. The walls aren't going to paint themselves.

Bachelorista takeaway: I'm guilty of pillowside scarfing

If Ben and Jerry want to join me in bed every night, it's my decision. Without Casanova hanging around, food lasts much longer. After a long day of work, I love knowing that the bag of overpriced blueberries in my freezer is right where I left it.

Bachelorista takeaway: The fingerprints on the thermostat are mine

In parts of the country, it's cold for many months out of the year (Hello, Alaska). If you're married in these areas, there's likely a good deal of commotion going on around the thermostat. She turns up the heat. He dials it down. For us Northern gals who are perpetually cold, this battle's right up there with the toilet seat.

Bachelorista takeaway: Our lounge routine is a secret

We can snore like a lumberjack and wake up with a mud mask on our face without scaring the bejeezus out of someone. Not your best in the morning Bachelorista? Put on your sanitarium sweats and give your stinky breath what it wants: another cup of coffee. Calling it a day at 3:00 p.m.? Sleep well, cocoa bean.

Bachelorista takeaway: No bitchin' in the kitchen

Just think, Bachelorista; you could be married to a man who returns home from hunting with Bambi strapped to the roof of his car. A smelly carcass in the garage, a loaded shotgun on the porch, and a bloody sink. Sounds like a romantic evening in!
Pippi pipes up: Messy is one thing, blood's another. Keep reading...

Bachelorista takeaway: He makes Daytona-worthy skid marks

You won't have to piece together the lunch combination your

hubby suffered through at Helga's House of Chili as you scan the hardware aisle for industrial-strength bleach to clean his J. Crew boxers. Bachelorista, you also get to avoid changing diapers and going to the ER because your toddler shoved a Lego up his button-size nose.

Bachelorista takeaway: We're first in line for everything

I love living alone. From hot water in the shower to my parking space, I have first dibs on everything around the house. Also, when I run out of something, it's not an I'm-going-to-clobber-someone surprise. This part of my single life is über heavenly.

Bachelorista takeaway: There's no TV script for this

Whether I'm watching Nashville or the season premiere of Downton Abbey, I don't have to outmaneuver anyone to control the remote. Here's a 9-1-1 call a Bachelorista will never make: "My husband's channel surfing drove me bonkers and I hit him over the head with my blowdryer. And now he's not moving."

Bachelorista takeaway: Mi casa es mi casa

As a Bachelorista, you won't have to invite your husband's brother into your home after his third wife throws him out, for the fourth time. It's your sanctuary and no one gets an invitation unless you're doling it out. Married ladies don't have the same luxury. To keep the peace, sometimes they have to invite people into their homes that they don't like. Some of these guests will find her fetching and pinch her in the arse. Chances are her husband won't cook their meals or clean their dirty sheets after they hit the road. When a Bachelorista gets an unexpected houseguest, it usually involves fun and, possibly, memory foam.

Bachelorista takeaway: Every 15 seconds, someone marries a slob

Like most people, I think housework is drudgery. But imagine doing it for an entire family. Listen, ladies, even if you spend a lot of time keeping things spotless on the home front, it's nothing compared to taking care of a family. Let's bow our heads in gratitude while our sanity is still intact.

When my writing is the most productive, my apartment looks like a war zone. I don't answer the phone or pick up the mail. I forget to eat. I don't know what day it is. During these times, I realize that focusing on myself is a luxury. And so I soak up and appreciate every minute of my free time.

Bachelorista takeaway: You could share custody of Ginger

Single ladies don't have to initiate a conversation about their pet that begins with "I want custody of Ginger."

Years before my friend Kristy's marriage fell apart, her husband Mark gave her a Golden Retriever puppy for Christmas. After they parted, deciding custody of Ginger became the Cos Cob version of WWIII. Bachelorista, you don't have to share Bam Bam or cart her across town for a visit with daddy. She's all yours.

Bachelorista takeaway: For me, it's nomatch.com

One of the most fun aspects of living in Bacheloristaville is creating a space that screams "me". You can decorate your shabby chic farmhouse without worrying about how the mister will ugly-up your decor.

Some time ago, I joined an online dating community. I spoke with a gentleman from the site on the phone. He told me that he supplemented his income by painting cow head carcasses and selling them as art. He'd buy the entire head from a butcher, then boil it down to the bone on his stove. Imagine coming home to that? If I can't get past a man's black leather couch, then there's absolutely no hope for this badass boiler. My man is signing a decorating Non-Compete, if I ever settle down.

PIPPI'S POW-WOW
Bachelorista Headquarters

The ultimate sanctuary restores, energizes, and inspires you. It's also a place where you have opportunities to grow. Living in a nurturing environment opens the door for play and experimentation. Whether this means trying out a new smoothie recipe, reading Abraham Lincoln's autobiography, or mastering a yoga pose, the more you find contentment developing yourself, the less you'll look to the world—and others—to make you happy.

Here's one of my favorite no-cost ways to transform your home into a sanctuary.

AWOG (Absent Without Guilt)

Updating the AWOL military term for Bacheloristas, this time-out is so rejuvenating that you're going to look forward to adding it to your schedule on a regular basis. What's the purpose of AWOG? It's to unhook and tune into yourself in a way that you can't during your daily routine. By leaving behind the stresses of work, relationships, etc., you're making a self-loving decision to just "be" as you fill up on head-to-toe nourishment in the comfort of your home.

What's the hardest part of AWOG? You're going to retreat from technology—and steal away from your cell, TV, computer, and anything else that puts you in touch with the outside world. As far as the rest of the planet goes, you're on a desert island. I know how tempting it is to fire up your laptop to read the latest work email or Facebook post. Think of this aspect of AWOG as un-boot camp.

Once you choose how long you plan to go AWOG (a day, weekend, etc.), stock up on nourishing food and plan no-stress activities like knitting, reading, meditating, or indulging in a bubble bath. In the days before AWOG, share your plans with a friend in case someone needs to reach you, and accomplish everything urgent on your to-do list. Chores are a no-no.

After our first AWOG, we realize that the world survives our absence swimmingly. Knowing this makes the next AWOG even better. Enjoy!

WRINKLED PAJAMAS

"When you realize there is nothing lacking, the whole world belongs to you."

– Lao Tzu

CHAPTER 3

THE GOD DEPARTMENT

Dear Bachelorista,

I remind myself often that the deity I believe in has a very good reason for keeping me on the playing field. Perhaps at the least, my life is a warning for women who don't want to be single over 40. On the day-to-day stuff, I'm grateful for just about everything–including inner peace, orange juice without antifreeze and the certainty of knowing that I won't catch hubby trying on my polka dot bikini.

More importantly, Bachelorista, you're blessed because you have the time to seek out what spiritually resonates with you and take it for a whirl. Last year, after transformative sessions with a shaman, many things shifted in my life. I quit my job, moved back to the Berkshires, and, from my kitchen table, I started a business. I'm glad I wasn't in a relationship at the time, because chances are he'd be toast.

Whether you believe or not Eve, you are beloved.

Monica

Bachelorista takeaway: You could give birth to the Anti-Christ
It goes without saying that your husband will blame your gene pool. He'd say something along the lines of "Didn't your Uncle Frank have severe problems controlling his temper?" And literally speaking, that's when all hell would break loose.
Pippi pipes up: You've been saved! You're definitely going to heaven.

Bachelorista takeaway: She's doing time for mankind
In Genesis, I love the way the Bible blames Eve for the downfall of mankind. So she ate the apple, big whoop. Here is how I think it went down before that fateful bite.
Adam: "Beauty before brawn."
Eve: "You sure you don't want to try it first?"
Adam: 'Nah, I'm good. I'm still full from lunch."
But let's just say that particular conversation never happened and Eve's guilty, as billions of people suspect. Then it would follow that all womankind carries her cursed seed. So why would any God-fearing woman deliberately bring a husband down with her?
Pippi pipes up: Beauty and brains before brawn is more like it.

Bachelorista takeaway: There's proof of heaven
God designed our female anatomy so that we could have great sex. There's no reproductive reason for women to climax (except incidentally in childbearing years: the more fun it is, the more women engage, the greater the chance of making a baby). Wouldn't it be obnoxious if guys were the only ones capable of orgasm? Then they wouldn't worry about satisfying us in that crazy-good way they do. Thanks, Papa God.

Bachelorista takeaway: Holy moly, Molly
People used to live much shorter lives and married much sooner

than we do today. Joining Jacob at the altar at the ripe age of 12 wasn't uncommon. Tween marriage? Ick. We're surely not living in perfect times, but in many, many ways modern women are blessed.

Bachelorista takeaway: Be fruitful and multiply in your own special way

God gave us everything we need to live a wonderful life. While there are many non baby-related ways one can be productive in this world, I get how challenging and frustrating it is to be patient when you have a biological timeline. But when you wait on your godsends, and enjoy the path you're on, you're much more likely to attract the things you desire (insert crying baby noise here). Besides, pushing the issue and settling down for the wrong reasons won't make anyone happy–children included. Bachelorista, don't settle. If you do, it'll make Pippi cry.

Pippi pipes up: It really will.

Bachelorista takeaway: Unanswered prayers have a silver lining

Every relationship that didn't work out wasn't meant to work out. Remember Frances Mayes, the lead character in the movie *Under the Tuscan Sun*? Diane Lane portrays a woman whose life turns upside down after her husband leaves her for another woman. After impulsively purchasing a Tuscan villa, Frances reinvents herself and creates a beautiful life in Italy. This lemons-to-Italian-ice story may not happen every day, but millions have metamorphosed into a more beautiful version of themselves after divorce.

Pippi pipes up: Diane Lane signed her filing to divorce Josh Brolin on Valentine's Day 2013. That must have been painful, but as the saying goes, you can't keep a good woman down. Like Diane, we deserve a wonderful, drama-free life.

Bachelorista takeaway: Kool-Aid kills

Your husband could suddenly decide to join a cult, become a Seventh Day Adventist, or follow Six Day Protagonists. While there's nothing wrong with spiritual evolution when your partner's on board, it's an entirely different thing if this new path involves guns, Kool-Aid, or mind control.

Pippi pipes up: If you have kids with a kook, you may live to regret that he has legal rights to your beloved children.

Bachelorista takeaway: You don't need to convert

Almost-engaged Charlotte York, one of my favorite *Sex and the City* characters, converted to Judaism for her other half, Harry Goldenblatt. Among other things, she attended religious classes, shopped at Jewish delis, and said a symbolic goodbye to Christianity by decorating a midsummer Christmas tree. The pair's future looked promising for an episode or two. That is until Charlotte put on her apron and with much ado made a traditional Sabbath dinner. During their meal, Harry was being Harry and snuck a peek at a baseball game on TV. When Charlotte followed Harry's line of vision to the Sony small screen, a Park Avenue holy war broke out. Charlotte, flustered from her recent foray into the culinary arts, ranted one of her most dramatic lines, "I gave up Christ for you. You can't give up the Mets?" After a few heated unpleasantries, this interfaith couple took a hiatus. Charlotte regrets her meltdown and tries to move on. Despite his hairy back, love prevailed and the couple got married.

Pippi pipes up: Bacheloristas, until you find your own version of Mr. Goldenblatt, live it up. You can do complicated later.

Bachelorista takeaway: Spiritual compatibility matters

Although I grew up Catholic, I no long practice Christianity. (Something tells me you've heard this before.) That's not to say that I think my parents' beliefs are wrong, it's just that for me, only one aspect of Catholicism resonated: God. I have nothing against Jesus, Mary, and Joseph, but since my faith in God has been unshakable since a young age, I didn't see any harm in just the two of us going off on our own. Besides, I've always been curious about how other faiths worship and love Him. Listening to Hindus, Buddhists, Jews, etc., talk about what God means to them is not only fascinating, it deepens my faith. I know it bothers my parents a little–especially my nun-educated, Irish Catholic mother.

Dating's another story. For me, connecting with someone on a spiritual level just never happened. Convictions in the God department run deep, so I don't find this altogether surprising. One man told me, "You've lost points in my mother's eyes because you're not Catholic." And for my part, I've shocked a few atheists by saying, "This isn't going to work, I'm sorry." If the guy wanted to know why, I'd tell him that I love talking about spiritual things. It's a turnoff to be with someone who doesn't believe in the existence of God. Besides, I know how it would play out with the atheist. We'd be doing something mundane like sitting in a café for breakfast when a hunky man would walk in with *The Law of Divine Compensation* tucked under his arm. As he settled down next to us, my eyes would bulge at the thought "OMG! He's a Marianne Williamson fan." Of course, I'd have to ask Lightworker about the book, we'd start a conversation, and Mr. Atheista would tell me that I'm drooling on my chocolate chip croissant. Bacheloristas, settling is never the answer–especially in matters so close to our hearts. Amen?

PIPPI'S POW-WOW
Time to Reflect

Whether we realize it or not, we live by the laws of attraction. Our thoughts have energy. When we focus on the good stuff and zero in on our blessings, we're creating the conditions to receive more of the same. More good stuff? Bring it on! Studies by Dr. Robert Emmons (UC Davis Psychology) reveal that practicing gratitude can increase our happiness levels by about 25 percent. Let that sink in, Bachelorista! This is powerful news.

If you already give thanks on a daily basis, I'm sure you love the mood boost. For those of you who'd like to begin this spiritual practice, here are a few ideas to get you started (there are many more online).

It's a Wonderful Life

For me, the holidays aren't complete until I see this classic movie. The troubled lead character, George Bailey, is visited by a guardian angel who shows him what life would be like if he hadn't been born. Taking the lead from a very grateful George Bailey (his life turns around in the end), this exercise will not only make you feel thankful, but it will also open your eyes to the lives that you've touched since you were a baby Bachelorista. Try imagining what your family would look like without you. Which friend would miss your support and love? Who would have adopted your pet and started the grassroots organization that's helped so many? After you think about the good that you've done just by showing up in the world, sit with those warm feelings a bit. Internalize them. Place your hand on your heart. Be still and know that your life is a gift.

Just You and Your Journal

If writing is your thing, a gratitude journal is cool. You can begin your entries with any iteration of "I'm grateful for." It's important to give yourself time to meander over different areas of your life. Blessings don't always jump out at you. Once you start rolling though, watch out, sistah. You may run off the page.

Imagine This

For some Bacheloristas, being grateful means tapping into their imagination by using what they've seen of their married friend's lives. If this is you, let's indulge each other a little. It's time to switch places with one of these ladies in your mind. You're now Mrs. Kay and the mother of two. Your day starts at 5:30 a.m. and it doesn't end until you and your husband turn off the lights at midnight. In between, there's waking the kids and getting them dressed, whipping up something nutritious for breakfast, making lunch, driving them to school, getting yourself ready, and squeezing in time for coffee. And that's just the early morning.

You'll also need to show up for doctor's appointments, arrange playdates, and pay gigantic household bills. Oh, and don't forget your son, Harry, needs a tutor because he's struggling with math. While we're talking about school, you have a PTA meeting on Thursday (note to self: Pick up a dozen doughnuts).

Now let's go to your workplace, shall we? Your boss doesn't understand when you need to leave at 2:00 because Tilly, your pug, is about to have puppies. He needs you to stay late, not leave early. Oh, yeah, and the report you did when you had the flu last week? It has a few gaps that need filling. With your present workload and the kids soccer games, reworking it will mean more late nights. Plus you need to fly out to Phoenix next Tuesday to present third quarter earnings to the board (note to self: Bring black suit to dry cleaners).

Back home, you haven't had sex with your husband, Bill, in two months and you worry about Alex, the 24-year-old Elle MacPherson doppelgänger with a crush on him at work. Balancing a career and family is ridiculously hard, and you beat yourself up over not giving your best to either.

Cake, huh? Another thing I didn't touch on here is that there are things mothers give up almost entirely—like consistent time to themselves and uninterrupted sleep. Bachelorista, this juggling act could easily be yours. While no one's life is perfect—single or married—there's always gratitude. Appreciate all the free time you have before your schedule explodes and your life becomes filled with responsibilities.

Phew, it's good to be you. Now go put on your heels and raise a ruckus.

Be Still
Be still and know that I'm with you
Be still and know that I am here
Be still and know that I'm with you
Be still, be still, and know
When darkness comes upon you
And covers you with fear and shame
Be still and know that I'm with you
And I will say your name
If terror falls upon your bed
And sleep no longer comes
Remember all the words I said
Be still, be still, and know
And when you go through the valley
And the shadow comes down from the hill
If morning never comes to be
Be still, be still, be still
If you forget the way to go
And lose where you came from
If no one is standing beside you
Be still and know I am
Be still and know that I'm with you
Be still and know I am

– The Fray

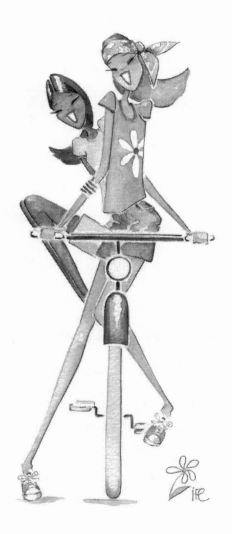

CHAPTER 4

HERE'S TO YOUR HEALTH

Dear Bachelorista,

Whether you plan on staying single for a lifetime or see yourself wearing a wedding ring someday, I'm here to remind you of the ways you're spared right now. Marriage is tough. Ask anyone who has taken vows. It's even more stressful raising a family. Managing household schedules and budgets, making sure everyone is well fed and healthy, keeping things hot on and off the mattress, and dealing with the fun task of blending your insane family with his is crazy hard. Putting everyone's needs before their own, women often ignore their health.

Sweet Valentine, you get to sit back and enjoy all the benefits your single status offers—including a less stressful lifestyle—and more time for laughing and exercising. You have everything you need to live a full and healthy life.

Live well,

Monica

Bachelorista takeaway: He's into late-night food porn

Eating healthy and staying at your goal weight is easier without hubby's Friday night sweet talk, "I'll have two XL sausage and pepperoni pizzas, and a side of garlic bread, please." I don't know about you but if it's in front of me, it's going down.

My friend Michelle is a hip single health fanatic in her 40s. When I ask, "What's for dinner?" I expect her to say a variation of "Wheat grass smoothie, Kombucha, and seaweed." One night, a young hottie (aka Ashtoni) she works with came to her apartment. After a heated makeout session, Michelle took out her blender for a quick nightcap. Ashtoni salivated at the thought of a fresh cocktail until he caught sight of the spinach, Amazing Grass Green Superfood powder, and frozen peaches. "You want a smoothie?" Michelle asked glowingly. Ashtoni almost lost his balance. When he recovered, he groaned "Eww, no." Fast-forward a few hypothetical years later to dinnertime in their house: One meal for her and one for the kid.

Lambchop, it's not always easy making healthy food choices. But since we don't need anyone's buy-in on the food in our cupboards and fridge, life's that much sweeter.

Pippi pipes up: Coo Coo, Cachoo.

Bachelorista takeaway: There's a healthy kind of doubled over

One of the funniest things about being single is hearing pickup lines. My personal favorite: "You're so fine, you make me want to go out and get a job." If you aren't enjoying your single life and living it up, what are you waiting for? Most studies show that married people are no happier than single ones. And what's more, women with kids are often less happy than their childfree counterparts.

Bachelorista takeaway: Horrormones are hell

Going through fertility treatments to have a baby with your

husband is no cakewalk. With hormones out of whack, savings dwindling, and no assurance that the daily shots will produce a baby, you're fortunate to avoid this loaded needle.

Bachelorista takeaway: The downside of naked knockabouts
Having sex may be good exercise, but if you're married, finding your sweet spot around frequency and the type of sex you have together may never get resolved. Plus, there are pressures like dealing with kids and financial problems that can dampen sexual appetites. Bacheloristas, without these stresses, your sex life has the potential to be amazing. If making love to your boyfriend doesn't feel right, you have an option your married sisters do not: throwing on your skinny jeans and hightailing it out of there.

Bachelorista takeaway: No nervous breakdown here
Whether she's worried he's being unfaithful, about to leave, gambling with their retirement savings, or taking drugs, marrying the wrong man could be hazardous to a woman's health.

Years ago, my friend Quinn's husband took a second job to get ahead of bills after she gave birth. With his new job located near his parents' home, he'd spend the night with them a few times a week or so the story went. Two suspicious parents and one private detective later, the truth came out. He had a girlfriend the entire time they were together. Apparently, his second job entailed keeping a bubbly brunette and her 12-year-old daughter entertained. They've been divorced for ten years now and Quinn still doesn't know if he fathered this woman's child.

Pippi pipes up: Whether married or single, relationships can be stressful. But when you're legally joined and things go wrong, your health may be jeopardized.

Bachelorista takeaway: There's a prescription for madness
Finding out you have a sexually transmitted disease is a lot worse when you get it from your husband. Especially when it's the same STD your best friend had. What's worse than finding out your other half and BFF are knocking socks? Contracting a disease from their horizontal escapades. It's an ugly topic, I know. But bad things happen to great ladies.
Pippi pipes up: The writing's on the wall. And it's not a love letter. You deserve better.

Bachelorista takeaway: Pass the Xanax
Rest easy, Bachelorista, you don't have to worry about your husband walking through the door with "I don't know why I've fallen out of love with you, I just have. I want a divorce."

There's something beautiful about people sharing their hearts and pain so that they can help others. Jennie Garth didn't have to speak about her divorce from Peter Facinelli. But with perfect grace, she did. What's more, she didn't pretty up the heartwrenching parts. Jennie showed millions of us women how an awe-inspiring reinvention is done.

Bachelorista takeaway: The bathroom is all ours
If you have to flush twice because of your low-carb diet, no one's the wiser. Plus you don't have to follow his stink bombs.
Pippi pipes up: Ewww.

Bachelorista takeaway: Your freak shows are private
After a gluttonous holiday season, my Lucky jeans don't fit. With buttons flying around the room, I wrestle them into submission long enough to shimmy over to the mirror. Feeling lightheaded and unable to sit, I drop and roll. I think my pants are on fire. I'm full of shame and feel lucky that no one, especially someone who is attracted to me, is around for this reality show.

Bachelorista takeaway: Game on, beyotch

It's easier for singles to make time for exercise. I used to work with Kim, an over-forty Bachelorista living in the Berkshires. In the winter this rock star comes to work an hour early so she can ski during her lunch break. In warmer weather she cycles 15 miles to the office a few days a week. Her fearlessness reminds others in her orbit to get off their ass—including me.

I don't have Kim's sports prowess and prefer to whack things, (Ping Pong or tennis, anyone?). The cool thing about being single is that we can squeeze in time for exercise without any to-do. The uncool thing is I seldom do. I carry around a beautiful bag of excuses. And I've honed the skill of matching the physical activity in question to a reason why it's not possible. Whether it's "I'm not feeling up to it physically" or "I need to relax more," I've become a black belt in tactical diversions. Because I'm on to myself, I've recently returned to the tennis court, huffing and puffing. I've made a promise to myself to stick with it.

PIPPI'S POW-WOW
Quiet the Critic

A month ago, I moved into a lovely Victorian apartment that used to be a candy shop (yum). The only downside is eight-foot mirrors against the entire back wall of the apartment. Ugh. I love that it makes the space feel more expansive and a bit like a ballet studio but eight-foot mirrors? I know myself; I have a tough inner critic. Every time I pass by, it's a challenge to suspend judgment: "Dude, your stomach looks four months pregnant." I'm learning to be kinder to myself, but I'm a work in progress. We women are hard on ourselves.

When I'm in writing mode, I often work until my eyes are bloodshot and I'm about to pass out. I know this isn't healthy. It's one of the downsides of living alone and being passionate about what I do. Since I'm not in a relationship right now, no one's saying, "Hey, Looney Tunes, come to bed." Although writing inspires me, it also does a bang-up job of kicking my ass. Not unlike the nights you party too hard and wake up with a hangover. It's tough on the body. What's worse than feeling crappy on these days? Our reflection.

For many of us, it's a challenge to find balance. Stepping away from our work to make a self-loving decision like exercise or getting enough sleep isn't always easy. It's work. It helps to have people in our corner who lovingly remind us to be good to ourselves.

My sister Nina struggled with weight issues. I first noticed a problem when she turned 11 years old. She began hiding food under her bed. It seemed bizarre to me, but I had no idea what it meant at the time. At 12, addiction wasn't a familiar concept to me so I kept it to myself–except occasionally when I'd quip, "What's going on under there?"

Each year thereafter, Nina either hit a plateau or gained more weight. This cycle continued for decades as everyone who loved her painfully watched her grow into a morbidly obese woman. I wondered how this could happen to my beautiful little sister? And why did she do this to herself? But no matter how much support we gave, we weren't getting through to her. After Nina turned 40, she began walking with a cane, and due to breathing issues, sleeping upright. After a bout with Bell's palsy, one side of Nina's face became permanently paralyzed. A few years ago, without the closure of a goodbye, Nina suddenly passed away from a glioblastoma hemorrhage. We were—and still are—devastated. Initially the thought "I wish I could have done more to help her" haunted me. Now, I've come to realize that she didn't want to change her body. She just wanted to be free of it.

While's Nina's life story is atypical, most of us struggle with inner demons and body issues—at least once in our lifetime. In the media today, women are bombarded with so many unrealistic images that it's a challenge to maintain a healthy body image. I'm not sure why we allow cultural expectations to cloud our self-image the way we do, except to say that we're up against mainstream madness and a formidable communications machine.

A while ago, my brother Werner began dating the most beautiful woman he'd ever met. But the more time he spent with her, the less romantic his feelings became. After a month together, he ended it. She lost her cool in a big way. Werner is an amazing guy, but if he can knock you off your center and flip your meltdown switch, you need to hold still and remember your worth. Healing the fractured parts of ourselves is work—I know from whence I speak—but if we are to become the courageous women we're meant to be, we have no choice. If all a woman brings to the world is her physical beauty, eventually she'll have her own rendition of Chernobyl.

It gives me hope that many women have quieted their inner critics. I love what Drew Barrymore said in response to a reporter's question about whether she felt rushed to lose her baby weight after giving birth to daughter Olive, "It takes time. Screw these impossible expectations. I'm doing it very healthy and sensibly. You must be nice to yourself. What kind of parent are you going to be if you're berating yourself in the mirror?" She went on to say: "I want to instill in her that when she's happy on the inside she'll be the most beautiful on the outside." Well said Drew. Ladies, let's take a cue from her. And remember, you are one of a beautiful kind.

"A fit, healthy body—that is the best fashion statement."

– Jess C. Scott

CHAPTER 5

FORCES AT WORK

Dear Bachelorista,

A year ago, I walked away from my editing job at a successful dot-com. Despite an incredible Statue of Liberty view, I sat in my cube on the 25th floor of a beautiful Hudson River building, feeling powerless and alone. I had once again tried to fit my 5'4" frame into a cookie cutter mold. I failed. But this time after leaving another unsatisfying job, I added a new skillset to my resume, *escape artist.* And that's when I decided to do what I should have done 20 years ago—listen to Confucius "Choose a job you love, and you will never have to work a day in your life."

After quitting my cube and saying goodbye to the New York City skyline, I'm doing exactly what I dreamt of doing: writing a letter to you.

Lock and load,

Monica

Bachelorista takeaway: Save the baby seals

Chances are you've either had a bad boss or you're in the trenches with one now. Ineffective leadership is an epidemic in the workplace today. Because so many of us have witnessed the damaging effects of a demotivating manager, we have the opportunity to succeed where they've failed. Whether it's communicating our vision in an inspiring way, fighting for resources, or simply treating colleagues with dignity, we have the goods within us to do better than they did. And what if we fail to live up to these things now and again? We make amends and do better next time.

One of my former bosses, whom I dubbed *Terror*, lived up to her name for dozens of reasons. Of the many people who worked for her, not one liked her as a human being. She had a stone coldness about her and a lack of humanity that I've never witnessed before in my career. In one of my meetings with her, I mentioned that I didn't feel empowered to do what I thought best for my team. Her response, "I don't believe you," shocked me. In that moment, an image of a baby seal flashed before my eyes. It suddenly dawned on me. I was the target of a corporate clubbing. Ouch! I cringe when I think about my former colleagues who still report to her. They are some of the savviest, most talented professionals in the industry who deserve to work their magic in a clobber-free environment.

Bachelorista takeaway: Postmortems are messy

I did a career autopsy recently, and traced my fatal move to the week after college graduation. Despite the fact that I wanted a writing job, I didn't have the patience for the paltry salary and instead decided upon a higher-paying marketing position. I made that compromise knowingly, but I never imagined that it would lead to 15 years of career unhappiness. With dollars signs on the brain, I went from one position to the next, and one city to the next. San Diego? Check. Denver? Check. Portland? Check. When things turned sour, I'd pack up a U-Haul and never look back.

Bachelorista takeaway: You don't belong in the backseat

You know that famous ballerina who gave up her career for her husband? Of course you don't because she sacrificed her dream for Prince Charming. Today, she's a divorced woman living on food stamps. She wonders who she could have been if she listened to her heart.

Bachelorista takeaway: Excel can make you loopy

Years ago, I took a position as an analyst because the company called the beautiful city of Monterey home (one of my smarter moves). The corporation spent thousands relocating me, and I couldn't wait to return to California. The first day of work came around and after an introductory meeting with human resources, a colleague dashed me off for training. After three days of mind-numbing instruction, I went to work on a mile-wide spreadsheet. The next day I woke up and did the same. I thought I'd lose my marbles.

Two weeks in, my boss and I were casually chatting at his desk when I let it slip that I wasn't good with numbers (What can I say? Excel made me loopy). Actually, it had nothing to do with aptitude; I just hated working on figures and percentages all day, every day. Staring at me, my boss let out a nervous, you-must-be-kidding-me laugh. Later that day, with my first paycheck in hand, I silently said goodbye to my teammates and left for the parking lot. I phoned human resources to apologize for my abrupt departure, confessing the job just wasn't for me. Months later, I heard they added a clause to their relocation policy: stay a year or return the money.

Once again, I failed to follow my inner voice. But as we all know, we can only run from ourselves for so long. The universe and I were playing the children's game "Hot, warm, cold." Like a strong-willed tyke who wanders off the playground, far off places were a distraction to me. And so the universe continued tugging on my cardigan.

Bachelorista takeaway: We have a greater chance of career happiness
With a family, you have built-in financial obligations. If the economy is tough, it's not that easy to leave a job you dislike for another. With considerations like salary, flex-time, and health insurance, a married woman's happiness isn't always a factor in her career decisions.

Bachelorista takeaway: This little piggy went to market
Another thing that happens when we don't listen to our inner voice is that we encounter fewer like-minded people. Many times that means we'll have to work alongside colleagues who operate with a different set of values. That's not to say that all is rosy when you're following your dreams, but when you share space with inspiring, fire-in-the-belly people, you're moving mountains, not tracking mud.

I had a boss named Phil (aka Little Piggy) who thought it perfectly normal to speak about his sexual escapades during departmental meetings. Each month, our work relationship grew tenser. Without letting on, I called company headquarters in Connecticut several times to ask about a job transfer. But because porn piggy didn't like my vibe, and had given me a so-so review, they responded "No, sorry." Crushed, I kept a low profile. A few months passed and I called human resources again because oinker crossed the "Oh, no you didn't!" line and said something foul about a female colleague. This time, I told the head of human resources everything. Within 48 hours, an entourage of corporate guys (mostly attorneys) descended upon our office. Since *Forbes Magazine* had just listed us as one of the top 100 U.S. companies to work for, they wanted this issue to go away. The day before the suits arrived, a woman from my department who'd just relocated from Long Island threatened my life. Our receptionist heard Miss Piggy's threat, "I'm going to kill you," and burst out crying. At 12:30 in the afternoon, our 50-person satellite office abruptly closed for the day.

Long story short, a female colleague sued Pigmeister, and I gave a deposition against him in court. My boss held onto his position. I, in my usual custom, kissed the floor with my face, and headed back home.

Pippi pipes up: Piggy wasn't permanently plucked from his pen? It's positively pathetic.

Bachelorista takeaway: You have reserves of talent

The inner work of finding and developing our gifts is super fun when we give ourselves time to explore what makes us tick. Pay attention to the things that come easy. What makes you giddy? What makes you forget time exists? Take it all in. And then celebrate what rises to the top.

Bachelorista takeaway: There are zombies in the conference room

Bachelorista, we're meant for great things. But if we trade our dreams in for something more glamorous, or because it's what others expect, things may work, but we will not experience bliss. If happiness is high on our agenda, then pursuing our life's purpose and sharing our gifts is non-negotiable.

One of the easiest ways to tell if we're in alignment with our life's purpose is to ask ourselves whether we're expending a great deal of energy on something that simply isn't working. If your career isn't fulfilling, shake things up and do what your heart calls you to do. I dare you. Besides, bored, caffeinated zombies (guilty as charged) aren't fun to be around. Be that woman who radiates happiness because she's living a purposeful life. She brings her magic into the world. And God knows we need it.

Pippi pipes up: Passion is the ultimate fuel. It can feed and energize every cell in your body.

Bachelorista takeaway: There's a downside to success
The more successful a married woman is, the more she risks emasculating her husband. Think about it. Diana, you don't have to worry whether hubby will graciously support your new CEO title—or secretly resent you.

Bachelorista takeaway: You can run but you can't hide
By the definition of insanity, that is, doing the same thing over and over again and expecting different results, I continued my certifiable path. I heard the warning, "Hey wild rover, why do you think nothing's working? Get off this train." But I didn't listen. I considered it a failure on my part that I didn't have the skills to color within the soul-sucking lines of corporate America. After meeting oodles of people who had similar experiences, I see it differently today.

Pippi pipes up: In the words of Marianne Williamson, "The best way to summon your true calling is to put yourself in service to God."

Bachelorista takeaway: Twenty-four/seven is complicated
Whether you're a venture capitalist or a third-grade teacher, you don't have to rush home to relieve the babysitter or worry about missing your anniversary dinner when you need to stay late. I know many successful married women (and mothers), but building a career is time-intensive and less complicated when you're a single gal.

Pippi pipes up: Don't be shy, Sunshine. Go make your mark on the world.

Bachelorista takeaway: Savvy networkers get ahead quicker
Corporate cultures are not always easy to navigate. Breaking into a new industry is just as challenging. Bacheloristas in the know use their free time to network. Whether it's going on informational interviews, or popping out for coffee with someone who has succeeded in your field, connecting with others will make your rise up the food chain easier. Once you storm the boardroom? Be a mentor and give back to other women.

Bachelorista takeaway: The fast track to London is yours
You can take the dream job in Canary Wharf without compromising your relationship. Or the travel-intensive sales position without fearing that your nine-year-old will burn down the house.

Bachelorista takeaway: We're still tiptoeing
How many men do you know who play small in the workplace? They don't have issues asserting themselves and owning their own power despite the fact that, on average, women are better educated. Until we own our strength in the same unapologetic way men do, and companies take a more serious look at why male executives outnumber female ones on their watch, we'll continue to experience inequality in the workplace. As for our part, let's negotiate better salaries, take more risks, and stop worrying about our likability. Perhaps we follow this mantra a bit more, "It's better to apologize than ask permission."

In some ways, little has changed since 1950: secretary or administrative assistant is still the most common job for U.S. women. Nationally, only 4 percent of men hold these support positions. I'm not saying there's anything wrong with these roles if this is what you choose to do, but I think as a gender, we need to look at why we're so willing to belittle our contributions in general—especially because our capabilities rival and sometimes exceed men's competence (a recent UK study from Barclays Wealth & Investment Management reveals that female entrepreneurs out-earn their male peers by 14%).

I've struggled with many issues in my life, but never when it came to going to battle for myself in business. It never occurred to me to forego the "negotiations game." To me, it's the juiciest part of business. I pretend I'm not worth much more than what you're offering because I know what the going rate is and that being in the arena means I must abide by these silly rules. So I say, "Yes" to the offer, but only after you lay down a good faith compromise – a measly $5k or $10k.

In my career, I've never felt fully compensated. I've marginalized myself in every conceivable way, but no matter how deeply I've failed or how humiliating the situation, I've always felt worthy of the best things in life–including a great career and a mountain of greenbacks. This is not because I think I'm special in any way, it's just that I know God is walking beside me. When you get me, you get Him, and so for that reason, I can't bring myself to settle in any area of my life.

PIPPI'S POW-WOW
Pursue Your Passions Challenge

We all know that living half-throttle isn't a recipe for success and happiness. If you've given up on your dreams, you may have abandoned your hope for both of these things. But I challenge you to listen to your heart and be courageous with your God-given gifts. Do the opposite of what I did. Instead of following the paycheck, follow your inner voice. Think about what your future self will say about your career choices. I'm pretty sure she'd be thrilled that you pursued your passions instead of settling for a humdrum career.

So Bachelorista, what are you waiting for? Let's get crackalackin. You don't need to have everything figured out before you start moving in the direction of your dreams. Baby steps are fine. And since there's no reason to go it alone, gather a support system around you, read, and get inspired. Go do what you're meant to do. Everything else is a waste of time when you think about it.

The universe supports our leaps of faith when we set out to follow our passions in life. But it's much easier to make a change when we have a positive attitude. If we believe in our gifts and in a better tomorrow, we have the mojo to rise up from the lull of mediocrity. Breaking free takes courage. It's scary. But if we say, "No" to a life-purpose adventure, the opportunity to create our own revival may never come again.

I love this quote by Albert Einstein, "The most important decision we make is whether we believe we live in a friendly or a hostile universe." What do you think Sarita? If you're not sure, allow me to believe in a friendly universe for you. And while I'm at it, I'm going to lift my glass and say a toast, "Bachelorista, here's to better days ahead."

"For any of us in this room today, let's start out by admitting we're lucky. We don't live in the world our mothers lived in, our grandmothers lived in, where career choices for women were so limited."

– Sheryl Sandberg

CHAPTER 6

IT'S YOUR MONEY, HONEY

Dear Bachelorista,

If you've got assets to protect, someone sniffing around your bank statements for a quick pick-me-up is unsettling. If on the other hand, you can't pay your rent, it's better to have no witnesses. But fortunes shift and Mr. I-loved-you-when-you-had-zilch might want to bump you off for the beach house and your Amazon stock.

Bacheloristas, many marriages break up over money. Wars are fought over money. And people go to jail when they steal money. You're lucky that you can spend your moolah any way you wish. It's lovely to be you, Soda Pop.

Bottoms up,

Monica

Bachelorista takeaway: You could be a modern-day Rose Maria Gnecco

You've probably never heard of Rose. But I'm pretty sure her husband's surname will sound familiar. Charles Ponzi, the Bernie Madoff of his day, made quite a name for himself back in the early part of the twentieth century. (As you've probably guessed, he's the original Ponzi schemer.) His life's work entailed dishonestly separating people from their money. He didn't seem to possess a single—or even irrelevant—redeeming quality: a sense of humor, a love of shelter puppies, or a patron of the arts. Nada. Even worse, nothing he experienced altered his path—including prison time, a parade of second chances, and the devotion of his wife. The craziest part of their story is that Rose knew of his criminal past before she got dolled up for the walk down the aisle. He probably knocked over a bank between the church and reception.

Pippi pipes up: Do you have a thing for bad boys with no moral compass? You might find yourself legally compromised someday. If the SEC charges your Gordon Gekko, you might be considered an accessory. A gold bangle is an accessory. You, Short Stack, are not.

Bachelorista takeaway: We can spend our money any way we choose

No need to hide the Saks bag in your car and wait until your husband leaves for a debt recovery seminar before you unbox your third pair of Manolos from the trunk of your Lexus. When the financial coast is clear, I enjoy shopping. I work hard and I like to treat myself. Explain my new shoes to a man? I'd rather go barefoot.

Bachelorista takeaway: It's a great time in history to be you

A little more than a century ago, single females had many disadvantages. Not only were they dubbed "spinsters" but women also didn't have as many choices as we do today—especially if they were born into humble circumstances. Whether she was coerced into a loveless marriage or she made a living as a servant (like the bottom-floor residents on Downton Abbey), the majority of ladies from this generation (and ones before) encountered overt sexism and fewer opportunities. Sugar Mama, it doesn't matter if you make $35k a year or $250k. The fact that you're financially independent means you have the freedom to live as you choose. Woo-hoo!

Bachelorista takeaway: Credit matters

When it comes to financing your dreams, your past and your FICO scores matter. If you marry a man who is financially irresponsible, it's going to impact your life, and possibly your credit worthiness. If on the other hand, you have bad credit, you can clean it up without any distractions.

Bachelorista takeaway: Lines get crossed every day

During a financial advice television program that aired recently, a woman caller admitted that she spent $48,000 of a $50,000 home equity line of credit without telling her husband. Her confession must have been difficult and probably resulted in some type of marital strain. Thankfully, for single women, your financial blunders are your own business.

Bachelorista takeaway: We live in a no-sponge zone

Eva is a friend of a friend who recently decided to cohabitate with her 45-year-old boyfriend. He didn't bring home a large paycheck but he had a steady job. After a few months she grew concerned because he stopped contributing financially. At 7:30 a.m. sharp every weekday, he walked out with his lunch box and returned in the evening with office stories to share. Suspicious of their new

monetary arrangement, she did a little detective work and discovered he had lost his job months before they moved in together. I think it's pretty safe to say that this guy's behavior is shady.
Pippi pipes up: Guess what? Dumbo got dumped.

Bachelorista takeaway: Your portfolio is safe

If you made more money than your husband, you could wind up paying alimony or part with property that's valuable to you. Think about all you've done to become financially secure. Money Bags, aren't you grateful that there are no he-bears clawing at your assets?

Bachelorista takeaway: People are funny with money

As a child, my mom told me about her friend Camille, who stockpiled cash in a secret account in case she needed money to leave her husband. I imagined that she had a fully loaded suitcase in her hall closet on the off chance her husband looked at her sideways. It's great that Camille prepared financially—kudos for her. But secretly piling up money sounds exhausting.
Pippi pipes up: Backup financial plan? Good. Married with one foot out the door? Not so much.

PIPPI'S POW-WOW

Who and what would you call into in your life if you had no limitations? Can you envision where you'd live, what you'd do for fun and how you'd make and maintain your wealth? Creating a dream board can help you get clear about these things. Whether you cut out magazine pictures or use Google images, it's super motivating to see your visual aspirations daily. Millions use these boards to manifest their dreams. You can too.

"True abundance isn't based on our net worth, it's based on our self-worth."

— Gabrielle Bernstein

CHAPTER 7

HAPPILY NEVER AFTER

Dear Bachelorista,

When it comes to joining our hearts with another, it's only worth it with the right person. This means that most relationships are just here to provide us life lessons (insert growl here). Never settle for good enough. You can do better, trust me. And let's be honest with ourselves: We know the difference between a punk who is going to cause us pain and a good guy who wouldn't dream of it. It's worth noting too, that even the best of men are not here to make us happy. That's a job for us, lovely lady. And the bennies you yield are amazing!

When I was young and insecure, I put up with ridiculous behavior in the name of love. I call this bungled time in my life "Doping with Dimwits." If someone asks if you're high because of what you're putting up with in your relationship, you're probably doping too. Spending hours trying to figure out why Dimwit 'x' does stupid thing 'y' is one of the symptoms of doping. Analyzing a doorknob is futile. Lara, lose his number. Cole Porter captured doping quite well in his song, 'Why Can't You Behave?' Bacheloristas, he wrote this song in 1948. If it were possible to change a man, we would have gotten wind of it by now.

It saddens me to see so many women making the same mistakes I made. I know the heartache that comes along with these lessons. If I could I'd wave a wand and take the hurt away.

Godspeed,

Monica

Bachelorista takeaway: There are roads better left untraveled

It's taken me a long time to get to this place but I have no problem saying, "Sorry, that doesn't work for me." It could work for the entire free world, but that's not my problem. As single women, we have plenty of opportunities to set boundaries. Sometimes a firm "No thanks" is the kindest thing we can do for ourselves.

A year ago, I met a guy on the subway. We exchanged a few emails and decided to firm up plans for dinner over the phone. When we spoke, I mentioned a cute French restaurant around the corner from my apartment that had amazing mussels. He asked if the broth in the dish had alcohol. I said I didn't know. When I inquired about his question, he confessed that he's a recovering alcoholic and even a dash of alcohol is troublesome. Since I'd been down that road before, I politely let him know that I don't feel comfortable dating men with any alcohol issues. I can bless the journey he's on (I know it's an excruciating one), but that doesn't mean I want to join him.

Bachelorista takeaway: You could hear, "You deserve better" for the rest of your life

A few years back, I took a road trip with my then-boyfriend, Rowan, and we had a spat at a restaurant. He had answered his cell phone at the table and then walked outside to chat with his "sister" outside. The longer I waited for him to return, the more furious I became. Ten minutes in, I had enough and walked out as Weird Beard casually sauntered back to our table. A cold exchange followed. A waitress who heard our banter watched us part in opposite directions. When I passed her on the way out the door, we locked eyes and she said, "You deserve better." It took her a few minutes of casual observation to throw up a flare. Rowan's cell phone etiquette wasn't what killed it for me, but the countless times he chose something else over showing me he cared.

Bachelorista takeaway: She's a stepmother

If you shack up or get married, you may be dealing with his children for the rest of your life. A few of my close friends are stepmothers. I've heard one or two pull-your-hair-out stories, but mainly it's a lot of work with little thanks. Kids will be kids, but when a child is not yours and resentful, it's messy. This is one gamble Bacheloristas don't have to take (at least for now).

Bachelorista takeaway: We could be married when Mr. Right comes along

He's everything you wish you had waited for. And guess what? He feels the same way about you. Looks like you and tight abs are about to break someone's heart. If you don't want to cause your husband unnecessary pain, be extra sure you're marrying Mr. Right, not Mr. Goodfernow.

Bachelorista takeaway: Doubting Thomas marries

One of the most surprising things I've heard in the last 15 years from quite a few men is that they knew on their wedding day that the woman they were about to marry wasn't the one. It's an alarming confession that when let out into the open doesn't make anyone feel better. It's disconcerting to think that my future groom could be up at the altar sweating bullets—not in fear of marriage, but of marriage to me! By the way, each of these men stated that they didn't want to disappoint their partners, so once the wedding plans were underway, they felt they had to go through with it. They hoped that their gut feelings were wrong. But like the men they love, women don't always trust their intuition and marry for the best reasons. Sometimes it takes an enormous amount of courage to do the honorable thing.

Pippi pipes up: Both Susie and Daniel deserve the truth and someone who loves them completely.

Bachelorista takeaway: We tango with everyday thieves
Mark, a golfer I dated for a year, grew jealous of the time I spent
with a gay friend. He thought I fibbed about this man's sexual
orientation. His suspicions were ridiculous and tiring. It got
to the point where I started lying to avoid a confrontation–it's
lame, I know. This wasn't just an unhealthy relationship; Mark
stole my precious time. But because I continued to show up, I
essentially gave him permission to rob me.
**Pippi pipes up: Bacheloristas, there's a world of difference be-
tween dating a green-eyed monster and marrying one. Don't
let a temporary lapse in judgment become a life sentence.**

Bachelorista takeaway: Marriage is a house of cards
Saying "I do" is a gamble. We never know how power dynamics
will play out between two people–especially over the long run.
Unresolved power struggles can undermine a partnership, making it vulnerable to a host of icky issues.
I'm still scratching my head over my parents' marriage. Despite an extreme flip-flop of power, they managed to stay together. For the first 20 years, my father held all the cards. In his
eyes, there was only one right way to do everything–whether
it was peeling a potato, dribbling a soccer ball, or saying the
rosary. His standards were exacting in other ways too. Deviat-
ing from a plan–any plan–wasn't an option. A storm barreling
through our area on the day we were leaving for a camping
trip? We still packed up our yellow station wagon, drove to the
Catskills, and set up tents in the pouring rain. When the holidays rolled around, let's just say singing Christmas carols wasn't
a join-in-when-you-feel-like-it kind of thing. We witnessed
more of the same when our relatives made the two-hour drive
to our Connecticut home. My father put orange construction
cones at the entry of our driveway so our relatives would have
to park on the street. Accidentally leaving tire tracks on our

perfectly manicured lawn? Dad wouldn't chance it. Because our driveway could fit everyone's car comfortably (it's a hard thing not to notice), he wasn't such a popular guy. None of this fazed him. He made the rules, and everyone followed–including my mother.

However, after 20 years of subjugating, Mom found her voice and things between my parents shifted suddenly. My reserved, soft-spoken mother slowly took control of the reins and has been the uncontested ruler of all things marital for decades. Every once in a while, my father makes a play for the wheel, but I think it's just an old reflex. Turns out, my mother is a tough dictator. That's what I call "karma alarma."

Pippi pipes up: Fortunately, the only flip-flops in a Bachelorista's home are the ones from Zappos.

Bachelorista takeaway: Creepy-crawlers spy on their wives
You could be married to a man who distrusts you to the point where he rummages through your emails and cell messages to check up on you. Insecure men make lousy (and sometimes dangerous) husbands. You know that cute skirt you love to wear? Tarzan may take issue with it when you leave for work in the morning. In his mind, your little A-line number sends a take-me-I'm-yours message to every man you see–including your boss, the plumber, and the neighborhood nice guy.

Pippi pipes up: Your intuition is spot on and just as telling as the red flags you may see in a man's behavior. By the way, you look awesome in that skirt.

Bachelorista takeaway: You could grow old with bossy pants
Years ago, my mother and I drove cross-country to visit my brother in San Diego. En route, we stopped at a Starbucks off the highway and just happened to be in line behind an elderly couple in the middle of a little spat. He wanted the raspberry

scone with sugar on top and the missus shot it down with a diatribe about his glucose levels. He responded with something that sounded like "bossy pants." They went back and forth for a few minutes. My mother and I lost interest in caffeine and were completely entertained by this couple. After some time, the gentleman turned to us, smiled, and said, "It's just the first hundred years of marriage that are the hardest." We laughed at this truism as they shuffled off.

Bachelorista takeaway: Regrets are not for you

When you're in your 80s and looking back over your life, you'll want to be able to share cool stories. Here's something a Bachelorista would never say: "I settled on a so-so career, married a man who loved me, and although I didn't feel happy, I made it work for the sake of our children." Please. No one wants to leave a legacy like that—not for themselves or their children.

Pippi pipes up: I love this quote by Daisaku Ikeda: "Everything passes. Both soaring joys and crushing sorrows fade away like a dream. However, the knowledge of having lived one's life to the fullest never disappears."

Bachelorista takeaway: Dr. Strangelove is lame

A woman I knew in college married a doctor. When I went to visit their "compound," I learned that her old man (Dr. Strangelove) had some very peculiar rules. The boat could only be taken out on Tuesdays and Thursdays; guests could only visit on Wednesdays and Saturdays, and on and on the guidelines went. When she finished rattling off his commandments, I waited for her to say, "No, I'm just kidding." She never did. I couldn't wait to get back to my own life and my itty-bitty studio. I've never understood why she chose to live like that. Bacheloristas, Dr. Strangelove is a real guy.

Bachelorista takeaway: Most players eventually marry

Let's face it: Men are hardwired a certain way, so blaming them for their biology is bonkers. If your man looks at other women, it could be that he has a healthy reaction to the opposite sex. It seems unrealistic for the man you had sex with this morning to shut down his libido at noon. If you're with a stand-up guy, his appreciation for womankind should fuel his sexual appetite for you.

If you think he's on the hunt for someone better, that's another story. Good guy with a healthy lust for life? Or player with monogamy issues?

Pippi pipes up: Before choosing flatware and making it legal, wait until you're 100% sure he's going to make a good husband—and the right one for you.

Bachelorista takeaway: You might set up an unfavorable chain reaction

If you settle down just to avoid the singles scene (or worse, to please someone else), you will most likely marry the wrong guy. And the woman meant for him marries someone who turns out to be the one you should have waited for. Ouch! Take a look back at your dating life. There's sure to be at least one train wreck you've avoided. Let's breathe a sigh of relief!

Pippi pipes up: Old houses settle, and it's not pretty. Don't be a house.

Bachelorista takeaway: We could share a fate with the first Mrs. Johnny Cash

I love the way Johnny Cash adored June Carter. Other women? Not a chance. His heart belonged to June. We all deserve someone who loves us like that.

Pippi pipes up: Only the best for the best.

Bachelorista takeaway: No one wants to be a member of club Crock-Pot

Here's a recipe you won't see on the Food Channel: Roll a lifetime of bad dates into one lousy relationship, add kids, house, and debts, and bring to a boil. Throw yourself into the pot. Serve lukewarm every day for 45 years. Yes, Patty Cakes, it could happen to you. Let's make a pact and put our Crock-Pots away until we're absolutely sure we're getting hot and heavy with the right guy.

Bachelorista takeaway: Your intended may like the idea of you better than the real you

In my 20s, I had a date with an architect. As I slid into his black BMW and got comfortable in my seat, I noticed a photograph jutting out of the air vent in his dashboard. (It was right in front of me, so I couldn't miss it.) I asked him about the picture and he explained that it's his just-finished dream home. From the blueprints and square footage to the Sub-Zeros and pool, he shared every detail of his new house. He also casually mentioned that he built a huge master closet for the woman he'd eventually marry.

The further we drove from my apartment, the more uncomfortable I became. I was hoping we'd have a low-key conversation over tacos and sangria. Instead Mr. Wifeshopper sized me up like a tuna he'd just wrangled from the sea. He not only confirmed the existence of marriage-minded men (hard to believe, I know), but he also managed to press all my buttons in the space of 30 minutes. His master closet plans had nothing to do with me. In fact, he didn't ask me a single question. Sure he'd steer the conversation to offspring before the dessert arrived, I made an excuse about a work deadline, and then my maracas and I made a beeline for the door.

We've all heard of men (and women) who marry just to perfect their image. To them, marriage is little more than a business transaction. Sounds like a solid marriage, huh? Solid crapola. **Pippi pipes up: Don't pack your suitcase just yet, Lucy Brown. There are better guys out there.**

Bachelorista takeaway: Women need wings

A healthy relationship requires balance. For Bacheloristas, that means enjoying a rich, full life. So when involved with a guy, Bacheloristas would never throw over their friends. No one wants to be that girl—you know the Houdini who meets a guy and disappears into thin air. While this particular magic trick is centuries old, it still shocks me. Women who are unable to make friends a priority are the very ones perpetuating the myth that all women are nothing without romantic partners.

So, Butterfly, do you have a married or unmarried Houdini in your circle of friends? Ugh. I can hear you booing her off the stage. And guess what? Dangling Donny is up there getting booed, too, because they're inseparable. Lady Houdinis are famous for bringing their husbands and boyfriends to a girls' night out (can you say awkward?).

My close friend Jill makes and keeps plans with her friends even though she's in a relationship. Like a true Bachelorista, she values our friendship enough to prioritize our time together. Because she knows she doesn't have to choose between friendship and romantic love, she gets the yummy benefits of both. The added cool part here is that her partner has the same breathing space.

Pippi pipes up: Ladies on lockdown forget there's a second act. This is the part of the show where Houdini's itty-bitty life with Flapper Jack gets too predictable, but no one's around to notice.

Bachelorista takeaway: This man makes me go, "Hmm"
He likes your hair long, his cropped like a greyhound, and large-breasted women. If he doesn't have three rows of Heineken in the fridge, he'll walk two miles in a storm to avoid watermarks on his Benz. He'll only eat Idaho mashed potatoes, and won't travel anywhere unless he's behind the wheel. He takes one shower a day and leaves four towels on the floor. He's content with one pair of shoes, two parts on his head, and overlapping toenails.
Pippi pipes up: Want his number? Just kidding. When couples tie the knot, they're not just marrying each other but also their odd quirks and preferences.

Bachelorista takeaway: Crazy likes you all to himself
When you're super attached to Mister Mine, and Mister Mine has his hooks into you, life can get unbalanced in a hurry. It takes healthy people to have healthy relationships. There are all kinds of crazy out there. Tinker Bell, if you're unattached, you're spared from these whackadoodles. Lucky you.
Pippi pipes up: Prison is for people who do bad things. Not lovely Bacheloristas.

Bachelorista takeaway: There are 51 states in America
If you've been through this depressed area of the nation, you'd never forget the female residents of Toxic Alley. They are strong and intelligent women who stay in relationships that are physically and/or verbally abusive. While we all hope this state disappears off the map, unless women walk away from relationships with hostile men, this territory will always be a wasteland.

Let's shed a little light on a guy from this area code, shall we? Packin' Jack doesn't come out of the gate swinging. He smiles charismatically, loves our mother, and wants to put a ring on our finger. He does all the right things until the day he doesn't. The first episode usually happens when our relationship is in its comfort zone. We're flushed, in love, and our pheromones are making us delirious. Then he shoves us, threatens us, or does some other Neanderthal thing, and we feel betrayed by everything that's good in the world. Cinderella, that's our cue to leave his crazy castle.

So whether he's banking in a Barney's suit or fishing in overalls, let's be kind to ourselves and remove these toxins from our atmosphere.

Pippi pipes up: Feeling emotionally and physically safe with someone is the minimum we should expect from a relationship. Shock, pain, and roller coaster rides are not byproducts of adoration. Let's clean up America and dump Toxic Alley men at the gate of Area 51. They'd make ideal candidates for military testing.

PIPPI'S POW-WOW
S.O.S

As hard as it is being single sometimes, compared to many aspects of life, it's a walk in Central Park—unless you're in a bad relationship. Then it's an unholy ramble into the wild. No one likes to worry about what's going to happen next. Will I get flowers or a screaming match? Will he be nice to my friends? How many beers will he have tonight? And on and on the insanity goes. Red flags and flares light up the sky, but somehow we pretend they are meant for someone else, a woman in a worse place than we are. But the wake-up call is for us. When a single woman stays in an unhealthy place, the universe takes notice. We wouldn't spend our precious time circling a dead-end street every day. But if we're in a destructive relationship, that's essentially what we're doing.

Let's take a closer look at how women in unhealthy relationships spend their time.

Toxic Alley Pastimes (Female Residents)

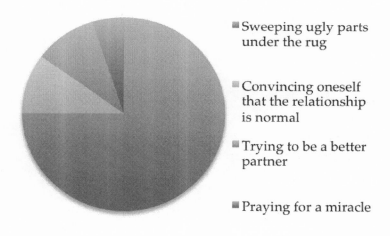

■ Sweeping ugly parts under the rug

■ Convincing oneself that the relationship is normal

■ Trying to be a better partner

■ Praying for a miracle

If you've had at least one time-sucking relationship, I'm sure you can relate to this chart. On some level we want to break free, but chemistry, low self-esteem, and sometimes history mucks up the waters, making it difficult for us to see clearly. In Bacheloristaville, when we can't find our way out of an unhealthy situation, we raise our hands for help. Like ships in distress at sea, we send out an S.O.S. That's when the women and men who truly love us arrive to show us a much better way.

HAPPILY NEVER AFTER

"Out of suffering have emerged the strongest souls;
the most massive characters are seared with scars."

–Khalil Gibran

CHAPTER 8

MUTUAL LOVE SOCIETY
Our Story in Numbers

Dear Bachelorista,

By now, you know how lucky you are to enjoy the freedoms you have. But without self-love, we may have time on our hands, but we'll fly by the good parts. We won't notice the flowers on the side of the road because we'll be too busy cleaning up our messes—the ones we created by making unhealthy decisions. We deserve the flowers and each blessing on the path ahead.

One of the great things about being single is spending time with our unattached girlfriends. As advocates for one another, we share experiences that make us sisters on a journey.

Together, our single lives tell an interesting story. The company we're in? There are tens of millions of single people in this country and billions more around the world. We're a growing demographic entering brand new territory and we're literally shaking up the grid. As they say, there's strength in numbers. But that doesn't mean anything unless we feel it on a personal level. (Numbers are little comfort to a single woman who needs a hug.) When we feel connected emotionally, socially, spiritually, intellectually, and physically, it's transformative. Since the world needs more kindness, why not start a mutual love society by supporting the Bacheloristas right in front of you?

In the meantime, let's ponder a few figures together, shall we? Bacheloristas like to keep things real so I'm sharing a few statistics that aren't pretty. But awareness–tempered by a belief in a benevolent universe–helps make us stronger.

You're not a number, Miss Bachelorista. But it's worth remembering that you're part of an adventurous tribe.

Stand up and be counted.

Mnica

Bachelorista takeaway: We're better together

According to the 2010 U.S. Census, close to half the population (100 million people) is unhitched. This is holy-shit news! This hasn't happened in our history until now. Where do we fit in? We're 45% of our population (over age 18). More accurately, Bacheloristas are the coolest part of the unmarried population in the free world. Now say this like you mean it "I'm in fantastic company."

Bachelorista takeaway: We're trending "single file"

Whether unmarried women simply have higher expectations about the type of man they expect to marry these days or they just want hot water in the shower, it's estimated that 17,428,000 women over 17 live alone (2010 Census). This number is dramatically different than reported a few decades ago. And in case you're wondering, today there are more single households than ones with Mr. & Mrs. Smith and little baby June.

Bachelorista takeaway: Freedom bells ring longer

Longer lifespans and later marriages mean that Americans now spend more of their lives single than they do married. This is the best of both worlds to my Bachelorista brain.

Bachelorista takeaway: Someday Gidget will get hitched

According to a 2009 report by the Centers for Disease Control and Prevention/National Center for Health Statistics, single women in the U.S. have an 86 percent chance of getting married before reaching the age of 40. Marriage-minded Bacheloristas, this is promising news for you. So stop worrying about the ring, and go plan something fun with your friends, and, um…don't read the next few paragraphs.

Bachelorista takeaway: Believe the fortune cookie

As we all know, half of all marriages fail. Now that's not a reason to shy away from marrying Mr. Right, but it's something to consider if Billy Joe's best asset is crammed into his tighty whities. You're not a statistic. Nor will you ever be. But few people win the numbers game. (According to the 2010 U.S. Census, the divorce rate of first marriages is around 50%; second marriages is 60 to 67%, and third marriages is 73 to 74%.) So why not be smart and do this math before saying I do? Find out what he's like on a bad day and then multiply it by familiarity.

As a society we're constantly bombarded with messages that say partnership is the key to happiness and success. If this were true, we wouldn't have crazy-high divorce rates, and all married people would feel blissful. I've learned to block my ears to conventional "wisdom." Care to join me, Dumpling? Over the years, I've come to find Chinese fortune cookies much more reliable.

Pippi pipes up: Like Billy Joe, these outdated messages have to go.

Bachelorista takeaway: The stigma lives on

Here's a strange statistic: Thirty-seven percent of women ages 18-34 say that having a successful marriage is one of the most important things in their lives (Pew Research Center, 2010). There's nothing worrisome about that. What's odd is that the percentage rose nine points since 1997–which is surprising given all that we know about modern women. I'm not saying that there's anything wrong with the desire for commitment and love. What I wonder about is whether this data suggests that single women are growing more fearful about the stigma attached to being unmarried. If this is the case, then we have a crisis of confidence on our hands.

Do women still cling to the myth of Prince Charming (PC)? Well, if men don't believe PC exists in some microscopic way within their better nature, then what hope do women have of manifesting a real life version of this fairy tale? One of the things I love about men is that they are practical. We need to give them props for being honest about what they're able to give us in the context of marriage and commitment. In fact, in the same Pew Research study I just referenced, males between the ages of 18 and 35 desire marriage 6% less than they did in 1997. These Romeos are looking at the same divorce statistics we are. Fifty percent odds don't inspire confidence, so why do so many women want to rush down the aisle? Perhaps if men were more hopeful about long-term relationships and women were more realistic, we'd find a happy middle ground. This isn't going to happen until women understand their true value–and power. Until they do, my heart breaks for every single woman out there who thinks she's incomplete without a partner. If she only knew...

Bachelorista takeaway: Not everyone peaks in their twenties
American women are entering marriage almost nine years later than they did in 1960. Recent studies reveal that there are fewer divorces among older, college-educated women. According to findings by the Council on Contemporary Families (2008), this demographic is the happiest married segment.
Pippi pipes up: Tory, how about this equation: Patience + matriculation = amazing dividends.

Bachelorista takeaway: The seesaw is lopsided
It's no big secret that the number of boys born in the U.S. has been declining for some time. However, since 1970, the trend has accelerated. Whether you believe experts who say the pattern shift is a natural byproduct of population dynamics or

you side with the scientists who claim that there's a connection between environmental stressors and genetic vulnerability (in men), it's a good idea to talk about what this means for future Bacheloristas. Today, according to the 2010 Census, for every 100 unmarried women in this country, there are 88 unmarried men. This isn't a reason to freak out. It simply means that if this gap continues to widen, we'll need to set great examples for the next generation of rock star Bacheloristas.

Bachelorista takeaway: More people are saying, "No, thanks" to marriage

About eight years ago, Pew Internet & American Life Project did a survey and found that more than 55 percent of the total never-married population had no interest in seeking a romantic partner. Whether this resonates or not, marriage is irrelevant for many of us today. According to the 2010 Census, 20.4% of men and 13.8% percent of women under 45 never married, a sharp contrast to 1970, when just 4.9% of men and 6.3% of women (of the same age) never married. When we think in terms of millions, these percentages are significant. Yowza.

Bachelorista takeaway: Voices still carry

If you've ever had this type of neighbor, you know that noisy can turn sad in a nanosecond. Years ago, I lived in Portland, Maine, in an apartment above a couple who were always fighting. One night, I heard my neighbor physically abusing his wife. Through the floor, her screams and sobs broke my heart. One of my neighbors called the police. I wanted to reach out to her but I felt afraid. I moved shortly thereafter, and I wonder what's become of her.

According to the FBI, one woman is beaten by her husband or partner every 15 seconds in the U.S. It's shocking that we've come so far in so many ways, but we have an incredible amount of work to do before violence against women is history. As you may know, domestic violence is the leading cause of injury to American women between the ages of 15 and 44. It's more prevalent than rapes, muggings, and car accidents combined. According to the U.S. Department of Justice, of the almost 3.5 million violent crimes in families, almost half were against spouses (84% of those being women).

Bacheloristas, I pray that your relationships are healthy—including the one you have with yourself. When we commit to making loving decisions for ourselves, our empowerment fuels everyone around us. It doesn't matter how many mistakes we've made in the past, the universe isn't keeping score (despite what fear freaks believe). As the saying goes, history is not destiny. When other women see your strength, it encourages them to find their own. For many, courage is contagious.

PIPPI'S POW-WOW
Mirror, Mirror Exercise

1. Walk to your favorite mirror. Admire what you see. Take in the curve of your nose, the shape of your lips, the color of your eyes. (Resist the impulse to pluck your eyebrows or judge.)
2. Now imagine that millions of single women are standing behind you.
3. Say aloud, "I'm in very good company." Let that truly sink in.
4. Take a few deep breaths. (If you still have the urge, pluck away.)

Single life can feel isolating sometimes—especially if the majority of people you know are either shacked up, married, or engaged. It helps to remember that you're not alone. There are single women all over the world who share your 'mirror.'

One night, years ago, I got dressed up and headed into Manhattan to have drinks with friends. En route to the Exchange Place PATH station in Jersey, a woman called out to me, "Walk that catwalk, girl!" I laughed and wanted to run over and hug her. I loved the dress I had on, but felt insecure about my toneless figure. Support from a sister? More please! I hadn't gone out since my sister's death, and this woman's kindness made my evening. Whether it's a small gesture or a big show of solidarity, let's be kind to each other.

"I define connection as the energy that exists between people when they feel seen, heard, and valued; when they can give and receive without judgment; and when they derive sustenance and strength from the relationship."

– Brené Brown

CHAPTER 9

LADY LIBERTY

O, Beautiful,

Who is luckier than you? You get to live as you choose and seize the day. Not everyone has that freedom. If life isn't working the way you wish, reinvent yourself. You don't need permission Firecracker; it's your constitutional right. Clear the decks of naysayers, throw unsupportive friends overboard, and stalk your dreams until you've willed them into being.

And make haste. The world is waiting on your particular brand of specialness. Now is a good time to light your inner torch and set your sails towards a happier tomorrow.

Watch out, sailor, she's heading your way.

Monica

Bachelorista takeaway: Inspiration is everywhere

If you're not in an anything-is-possible frame of mind, it helps to remember that someone walked in your shoes once and went on to become a huge success. Whether it's an against-the-odds type movie, a good biography, or a conversation with someone who inspires you, there are powerful and motivational resources all around you. Every day, people around the world overcome gigantic obstacles to become kick-ass successes. There's no reason why you can't too.

I've allowed my circumstances to get the better of me many times throughout my life. From a young age, my parents voiced, "If you want something in life, then work for it." Many years ago, that meant paying my own way through college. Emotionally and physically, I felt overwhelmed. During these times, my grandmother, Norah, often encouraged, "You are capable of great things, Monica." To remind me of life's possibilities, she pointed out the plights and accomplishments in our family. If she could lose parents and siblings at a tender age and then board a ship to America, surely I could keep my world afloat. If my German grandfather, Albert, could find his way home after five years as a prisoner of war in Siberia, surely I could pick myself off the floor and keep moving. If my great grandmother Marianne Murphy-O'Shea could graduate college in the late 1800s, marry a captain of industry, and become a mother of six, surely I could graduate college 100 years later. Norah's words both comforted me and gave me a kick in the pants.

Bachelorista, anything is possible. Limitations—like smoke and mirrors—have no power over us unless we believe they are real. Practice gratitude and shift your perspective, and the world will appear at your feet. Your spirit is unstoppable. Tap into that strength and believe.

Pippi pipes up: As much as Bacheloristas love to have fun, they draw the line at pity parties.

Bachelorista takeaway: Speak from your heart

At the age of 22, I dated Frank, a family friend. After a few months together, my birthday rolled around. He forgot my special day and I took it personally. I didn't know how to handle my feelings at the time, so I reacted childishly (seven-ish) and decided to strike back: I kissed another man in front of his roommate (I know, it totally lacks imagination). Of course, it backfired. Instead of making him jealous, he didn't want to see me again. I felt devastated. One night, I searched for him in all the places we went together. The more I sought him out, the more emotional I became. Thankfully, my intuition kicked in and I called home. My sister Susan answered the phone. She could tell that I had one too many drinks and sounded down. In a very sweet voice, she said four little words I'll never forget, "Just come home, Moni." Her words cut through the pain I felt and possibly saved my life (drinking and driving, so not proud of that). How often we underestimate how words affect others.

Bachelorista takeaway: Be generous with praise

When we hold a space for another woman's greatness, we're co-creating a more loving world. Your talents bless everyone. As do mine. There's no competition between us because we each have our own paths to follow. If you're tripped up by someone's fabulousness, it's a sign that you're not focused on your own life and have lost touch with the unique gifts you bring to the universal table. On the table, there's a feast of delicacies. When things play out between us and we're following this girl code, what I bring nourishes you and what you whipped up fuels me. I can tell you how delicious yours is because it takes nothing from me to call out something you do smashingly well.

What if no one sings your praises? Ask yourself how well you support other women, then tap into the adoring fan within yourself. Believe in your gifts and worthiness. I know it's not easy to call out someone's ability when you're feeling insecure– especially if you don't like this person. But their successes pave the way for others, including budding Bacheloristas. And just as importantly, the universe rewards kindness.

By the way, we're lit up and radiating from a soulful place or we're not. I've met super-accomplished women who have all the goodies of success but none of the grace. Thankfully, that's not your story, Bachelorista.

Pippi pipes up: How great is it to see shooting stars zoom across the sky? Pushing through the atmosphere, overcoming a world of resistance, they show up for us and blaze their light. They've come a long way to remind us of the infinite possibilities lying in wait within ourselves. Hmmm. Kind of like the women all around us.

Bachelorista takeaway: We're rebranding feminism

When a product name is tarnished in the corporate world, it's often rebranded. After radical feminists came out swinging in the late 60s and 70s with anti-family, anti-men, and sometimes non-inclusive messages, they polarized the nation and gave all feminists a bad name. They also redirected everyone's attention from the real issues of inequality and marginalized the work of instrumental pioneers in the women's movement.

Just how do we move on from this? Perhaps we need a little imagination. Picture a revolutionary scientist whipping up a new gender in the lab. She'll mix together the yummiest qualities of him with the tastiest of her (maybe add a few chocolate chips), and the newbie gender would hit the streets. The man/woman monopoly would officially end, and Lady Jane and Dashing Dan, fearing extinction, begin to see each other in a new light. She ponders coyly, "He's not that bad." And he looks at her and thinks (drooling), "She's cute." Together, they wonder why they made such villains of each other.

Until that particular news hits *The New York Times*, men and women are all we've got. Why not focus on the good? Who cares about bitter and angry extremists like male chauvinists and women who emasculate men? Let them sleep alone. Bacheloristas keep much better company. As for women supporting other women, let's remember what Madeleine Albright said in her keynote speech at the 2006 Celebrating Inspiration luncheon, "There is a special place in hell for women who don't help other women."

Pippi pipes up: In the dance between men and women, let's forgive the mistakes we made yesterday and use this moment to focus on the divine in each other. If we can do this, we're destined to bring the music back and witness miracles in our lifetime.

Bachelorista takeaway: Be the brave example

People look up to you. You may not know this, but they do. You think that you're just living your life, but to them, you are the embodiment of what they hope to be. That doesn't mean you need to be perfect. God knows, the world doesn't need another robotic blonde.

Bachelorista takeaway: You have the makings of a legend

What is stopping you from being the heroine of your very own adventure? Dare to dream big and create a life worthy of your talents. By the way, who is your biggest fan? Well, Leading Lady, as much as I think you're fabulous, it's got to be you. The role of a lifetime is yours for the taking.

Bachelorista takeaway: We've got the green light

In a previous job, I had a conversation with Ivy, a female colleague. We were discussing her family (she's married with kids) when I asked her if there's anything she missed about single life. She mentioned a happy hour invite that circulated around our office and how she would have loved to go. But because of her family obligations, she couldn't even consider a last-minute invitation. Getting the green light meant coordinating sitters, rescheduling playdates and determining how her husband's work day figured into this midweek schematic. She said that she gave up her spontaneous lifestyle in two stages—first after saying her vows, and second after giving birth to her daughters. I've considered how the other half lives before but never in a holy-shit-this-could-be-me context. I'm not saying that happy hours are important, but freedom to do what you want is huge in anyone's book. I walked back to my cube that day with a renewed appreciation for my life.

Pippi pipes up: You're free, woo-hoo!

Bachelorista takeaway: Shine on

You can begin your MBA, start a business or accept a new position without worrying how the peeps at home will deal with your new schedule, confidence, and energized brain cells. Rocket scientists don't become who they are without putting in the work.

I met my twentysomething friend Ruth at a dot.com we worked for in Jersey City. We sat on opposite sides of a cube. Ruth's more than whip smart—her brain works like a lightning speed computer. Consequently, she's a few steps ahead of everyone most of the time. But she's also one of the hardest working and fun ladies I've ever met. Under extremely difficult circumstances, she paid her own way through college and was recently accepted into Harvard Business School. Harvard is lucky to have Ruth. Bachelorista, define your dream, then put it into motion. Eventually, hard work pays off.

Pippi pipes up: You'll know when you've arrived. People won't be able to take their eyes off you.

Bachelorista takeaway: Have no fear

Ah, independence is a beautiful thing. Despite the unpleasantness of occasionally falling on our faces, we have many, many opportunities to grow and take responsibility for our own actions. We can't hide behind anyone—or blame our other half for missteps we make: "Diana, I'm so sorry you lost your savings because of the stock I recommended. My husband believed it couldn't fail. Will you need to move in with your parents?" Without a human shield, we are forced to clean up our own messes and evolve—as painful as that is sometimes.

Of the m-a-n-y mistakes I've made in my life, there's one that stands out as my most embarrassing moment. If someone had been beside me at the time, I wouldn't have learned what I did. Which is this: I don't want anyone to stand in the way of a lesson I need to learn (as tempting as it may be). The good stuff that comes along with the life lesson is what I'm after.

My blunder occurred four years ago while I was staying at my parents' home in their adopted state of Tennessee. At the time, there was a funny movie just released in theaters. I invited my 70-year-old father to come see it with me, and we decided on a matinee. He'd just gone through a tough time with cancer and I wanted to cheer him up. At the last minute, my mother decided to come along. She invited a senior couple from her church choir. The five of us met in the theater lobby, and then settled into our red velvet seats in time for previews.

When Sacha Baron Cohen lit up the screen as the gay Austrian fashion journalist Brüno, I wasn't too concerned because, well, we're all adults. A few minutes later, the movie took a wild turn down a sex-filled "back-alley." As graphic images moved across the screen in slow motion (um, not exaggerating), I froze in my seat and prayed for the scene to change. But it wasn't to be. One depraved vignette gave way to another even raunchier. When I found the courage to look over at my mom, I opened my hands in a Jesus pose and whispered loudly, "I'm sorry." Sitting in the seats beyond my mother were Mr. and Mrs. Rose and my dad. In the dark, I couldn't gauge how the guys were doing. But after catching a few words in the exchange between my mom and Mrs. Rose, I knew it wouldn't be long before they grabbed their coats and left–which they did moments later, visibly annoyed.

And then it became more awkward. My thoughts raced. Do I walk out of the movie in solidarity with the ladies? Or stay slumped in my seat waiting for my dad and Mr. Rose to leave? With my motto being "no man left behind," I sat there paralyzed for what seemed like hours until a close-up of Brüno's penis swung left to right across the screen. His pelvic gyrations were my salvation because my father took this cue to say, "This is crazy," and the three of us awkwardly got up to leave.

Further embarrassment awaited in the lobby. The theater manager summoned by my mother and Mrs. Rose stood across the counter from them processing two ticket refunds when we joined them. No one made eye contact. After an uncomfortable silence, I apologized to everyone, "I'm so sorry, I had no idea." Shamefully I walked out of the theater into the hot Tennessee sun. I felt scorned like one of those corrupt characters in the Bible–but I couldn't decide between Jezebel, Mary Magdalene, or Potiphar's wife.

Back at the house, despite the early hour, I didn't see my parents again until later the next day. The following year, I saw the Roses at my parent's wedding anniversary celebration. I had a flashback to Brüno and thought "Eww; I'm still trying to forget images from that movie. What chance do they have?" Lovely ladies, that's my Bible Belt blunder. I'm sure you have your own humdingers.

Without anyone whispering in our ear, "Hey, crazy lady, your idea is whacked," we're kind of swinging in the wind like Brüno. Growing and evolving may sting here and there, but the upside is that we learn to stand on our own. All this growing-up business is tough. A cold Stella, anyone?

Pippi pipes up: I'm thinking more Amelia Bedelia than Jezebel.

Bachelorista takeaway: Keep your passport handy

You can join the Peace Corps without consulting Paulo. Bacheloristas can say, "I hope you take quarters, I need a one-way ticket to Bangladesh, please."

Susie, one of my friends in the Berkshires, recently spent three months in South Africa to donate her time and talents to an orphanage. Because she's free to say, "Yes, I'm coming," Susie's making a difference in the lives of many children. Volunteering is a win-win for everyone, and typically easier for Bacheloristas.

Bachelorista takeaway: Check off that bucket list

You can take up skydiving without hitting a sour patch with your partner. If you have a rough landing, you won't see shorty pants pacing your hospital room recycling, "I told you so, now our health insurance is going to go up!"

Bachelorista takeaway: Use your power for the greater good

Our voice is powerful. Let's use it to protect the people, places, and things we love and value. Before we find courage to defend others, we need to stand up for ourselves. Sometimes this means that we'll need to challenge the status quo. Bacheloristas are strong and understand their own power in co-creating a more fabulous, tolerant world.

Bachelorista takeaway: Pursuing perfection is loco

Holding ourselves to ridiculously high standards in all areas of our lives is cuckoo. Expecting others to act a certain way is bonkers too. I'm not sure why women struggle with this in such a huge way, but since all of us fail the perfection test 100% of the time, I don't know why we keep trying. If life itself is a beautiful mess, why do we think we'll outwit the universe and pull off the coup of all time? Plus, perfectionists aren't having fun.

Once upon a time, I strived for perfection in my writing career. But after a decade, I realized how silly that is—especially because grammar challenged me throughout my education. I found the endless rules frustrating, as well as the nitpicky exceptions to those rules. (My editor will confirm, I'm only slightly more informed today.) I think people assume writers have this stuff down. When someone asks me a grammatical question, I use Google to find the answer. It's much trickier when they suddenly appear at my desk. Argh.

Since making mistakes is unavoidable, it's good to have a plan in place when we screw up (i.e. apologize, learn the lesson, channel our inner awesomeness, and move on). Last night, I messed up and acted unkind to someone. After realizing my blunder, I felt like the biggest jackass and apologized. It took a while to let that icky feeling go. If you're a kind person and you treat someone poorly, it's not supposed to feel good.

Hopefully, we love ourselves enough to define ourselves by our best moments and the people we are 85% of the time, not by the things that make us cringe.

Bachelorista takeaway: Testosterone is distracting

As a group, men are beautiful creatures. Mixed into a foreign, heady package, their strength and masculinity instantly change the energy in a room. When a man I'm attracted to stands before me and enters my physical space, every cell in my body stands at attention. I can't help but study him: the plump of his lips, the chocolate pools in his eyes, the razor sharp cleft in his chin, his not too big or small biceps. Chemistry is intoxicating. Even now, I'm distracted writing about why men are so distracting. The images of a few men I know are popping into my head. Yum.

I've always felt this way. My first kiss didn't take place in the back of a tween school bus. It happened in 1970, at the age of five. My same-age childhood crush, Tommy Logan, lived four houses down from me in East Meadow. We often stole away from friends, huddling alone in our favorite hiding place—a lilac bush around the block. Tommy first kissed me there. Imitating our married neighbors, we closed our mouths tight and pressed. And we practiced. I didn't love Tommy because he looked cute or because he had caramel-colored freckles. I loved him because he acted fearless, and because he chose me, in all my Pippi Longstockings wildness, over the other pigtailed girls on our street.

The summer before kindergarten, Tommy and I had no appetite for socialization. Running through the streets, playing on swings, standing united against the neighborhood bully, we didn't want the adventures to end. On some level we knew that school would forever change us. To us, the whole forced-to-go-to-school thing seemed un-American. We thought of phoning President Nixon, "What about our rights as young kids of New York?" But even at 5 years old, we knew it would be futile. Instead, in the weeks leading up to the first day of school, we came up with a more localized plan: Tommy would jump on Mrs. LaRuffa's back and I would attack her legs. When the first day of kindergarten rolled around, I wasn't sure if we'd chicken out. But when I saw Tommy leap, I dove at Mrs. LaRuffa's legs— and we created a hallway commotion. Tommy and I held onto her until another teacher upended us. After the stunned Mrs.

·

LaRuffa regained her composure and gathered her papers from the floor, she furiously sprung into action. She took us by the ears (they were allowed to do this back then) and we were exiled to the principal's office. We had been so excited about our showdown that we didn't give much thought to the aftermath. But as we sat in an unfamiliar office, in front of an unfamiliar man, with our tussled but new first-day-of-school clothes, we realized the gravity of our booboo. Mr. Moore called our parents to retrieve us. My mother and Mrs. Logan arrived together. I remember seeing Tommy walk off with his mom. I wanted to ask him if he regretted what we'd done. The next day, Mrs. LaRuffa separated Tommy and me in class. On the home front, Tommy went back to his boys and I tried to forget him. I felt completely heartbroken for the first time in my life.

A few years ago, my parents and I visited our old neighborhood in East Meadow. We stopped in to see Mr. and Mrs. Logan. As we sat and caught up in their living room, I wondered what type of man Tommy became. I scanned the family pictures on their mantel but I couldn't identify Tommy from the other boys-turned-men. It occurred to me that it didn't really matter. Those memories were mine.

Fearlessness will always be sexy to me. Perhaps when a courageous co-conspirator arrives and takes me as I am, I'll have something more relevant to say on the subject.

Drumroll, please.

Bachelorista takeaway: You can show the world—wait for it—what happy looks like!

I wrote *The Life & Luck of a Bachelorista* to unearth all the good single life offers and connect with cool ladies like you. I hope you love your life as a single woman. If not, there's no better time than now to begin.

PIPPI'S POW-WOW
Move Mountains

There is greatness inside of you. You have reserves of talent that enable you to live a deeply satisfying life. Whether you've succeeded in realizing most of your dreams or you're still trying to figure out what you're good at, we can all make the world a better place to be.

One of the easiest ways to do this is to share your gifts with others. I'm one of those people who believe that a higher power is too formidable an ally to ignore. If you let it, spirituality can play a huge role in helping you fulfill your dreams.

In my 20s, I read something by Iyanla Vanzant that changed my life. She said, "Your blessings have your name on them." Her words opened my eyes. What a relief! I don't have to worry about getting my good? Hallelujah! Because of Iyanla, Marianne Williamson, and others like them, I've learned to trust the universe and enjoy my life in a deeper way.

Before leaving corporate America, I worked with a shaman who introduced me to soul retrieval—a life-changing experience that not only heals the hurts of the past but also guides your future steps. I know this might sound hokey to some of you (I only half-believed it in the beginning too), but it transformed my life in ways I'd never imagined. When you do what you're meant to do on this planet, the universe has many divine gifts to share. I hope right now you're getting your good. If not, there are many people who can help.

10 Ways Bacheloristas Can Make the World
A Better Place

1. Follow your dreams. People need that thing you do so well. Also, your talents have a rippling effect. When we're tapped into our soul's purpose, we encourage others by example.

2. Give back. Volunteer your time to a charity, or touch a life right in front of you. When we're not on our cell phone or distracted by our own lives, we'll see many ways to help– even if it's just to hold the door open for a stranger.

3. Say a kind word to people on your path. They may be going through a dark time and your encouraging words can make a difference.

4. Ask for help in healing the places inside you that feel broken. Happy people are magnetizing, and their energy is contagious. If we're coming from a place of love when we're out in the world, we contribute to world peace. Why not look people in the eyes and smile like you just won the lottery? In many ways, you have.

5. Show up, even when you don't feel like it. Why do this? Because you, dear Bachelorista, make a difference wherever you go in the world. You just can't help it. And as we've all experienced, when we take that step of faith and show up for the people around us, our heart, mind, and soul play catch up.

6. Become a great listener. Giving people our full attention is a great act of kindness. People are hungry for us to listen to them.

7. Teach others the things you do well. There's nothing more generous than sharing our gifts.

8. Have the courage to be yourself and bring your true self out to play wherever you go. And because there will always be people who judge, let's internalize these words by Brené Brown, "Don't try to win over the haters; you are not a jackass whisperer."

9. Be positive. Good energy creates more of the same. Focus your light on the blessing, and don't worry about the rest. Let the media focus on the negative. By tuning into the good in people and in a situation, we're spreading the message of hope and possibility.

10. Give thanks for all the amazing things around you (and within you) and let your gratitude fill the air. Through the act of appreciation, we're divining a more inspired world.

"Keep your best wishes close to your heart and watch what happens."

– Tony DeLiso, *Legacy: The Power Within*

THE BACHELORISTA'S PLAYBOOK

Rules. Most of us don't like making them, and following them is a bore, unless we absolutely have to or the rules are so much fun that we don't want to miss out. But then they'd probably be called something more enjoyable–like a playbook. I've gathered the top takeaways from this book to remind you that you're loved and deserving. Make a splash, Bachelorista.

1. A Bachelorista feels empowered.
2. A Bachelorista loves herself.
3. A Bachelorista celebrates her single life, unapologetically.
4. A Bachelorista remembers she's in fantastic company.
5. A Bachelorista believes in herself and in a benevolent universe.
6. A Bachelorista pursues her dreams.
7. A Bachelorista makes self-loving decisions.
8. A Bachelorista respects herself and others.
9. A Bachelorista possesses a positive attitude.
10. A Bachelorista knows fairy tales are fiction and that real life is more fun.
11. A Bachelorista knows when to say hello and goodbye.
12. A Bachelorista protects her heart, mind, body, and spirit.
13. A Bachelorista embraces her lack of perfection.
14. A Bachelorista believes in and develops her talents.
15. A Bachelorista trusts her intuition.
16. A Bachelorista fights for what she believes in.
17. A Bachelorista feels energized by life's possibilities.

18. A Bachelorista knows how to lovingly say "no."

19. A Bachelorista practices spirituality and gratitude.

20. A Bachelorista values her health.

21. A Bachelorista trusts love.

22. A Bachelorista believes in the equality of all people.

23. A Bachelorista shows up and contributes to the conversation.

24. A Bachelorista is patient and knows that her blessings have her name on them.

25. A Bachelorista tosses out timelines that don't work for her.

26. A Bachelorista supports other single women.

27. A Bachelorista takes responsibility for her mistakes, learns from them, and moves on.

28. A Bachelorista knows that marriage won't make her feel any happier than she is right now.

29. A Bachelorista forgives herself and others.

30. A Bachelorista leads by example, uplifting other single women.

31. A Bachelorista reinvents herself when she's unsatisfied with her life.

32. A Bachelorista values community.

33. A Bachelorista asks for help when she needs it.

CLOSING THOUGHTS

Marriage, like single life, isn't a fairy tale. But the fact that many women believe that becoming a member of club hitched will make them happy is what's tripping everyone up. Flipping the switch on the happily-ever-after lie won't happen until singlehood is appreciated, not pitied. Perhaps that means we need to stop envying our sister for landing a Park Avenue lawyer and instead ask her if this man enriches her life in a non-material way. Let's save our hearts for the good guys—the ones who know how to revel in our love and return it to us passionately.

Internalizing the Bachelorista perspective means letting go of timelines along with everyone else's idea of happiness and celebrating life as it is right now. It doesn't mean we opt out of relationships or love, but that we turn down the noise and release the expectations that restrict us. Let's stop dining on the crumbs of another generation. Their outdated beliefs about singlehood and marriage have no substance, and therefore no sustenance. What's worse, conventional wisdom chokes instead of liberates. It doesn't heal our heart, it steals our voice. For Americans who have made an occupation of spreading hate and intolerance in this country, let's say a prayer for peace and push back. Quiet, disqualified, and living in the past is no place for a Bachelorista. You, Buttercup, have new roads to travel, shoes to try on, and plenty of sun around the bend.

My fortune-teller knew her stuff. Life had better plans for me. But until I believed that my gifts had value beyond my little world, life wouldn't open up. The process of coming into my own was a long and clumsy one. But it's worth it.

Some people are born with a very strong sense of who they are—like my grandmother Norah. This five-foot-tall Irish spitfire had a Texas-size ego. She came to the states at 20 years old, met my grandfather years later, and raised my mother and her siblings on Manhattan's Upper East Side. I grew up listening to stories of their lives. One of my favorites happened in the 1950s. After school one day, my mother and her two sisters were walking in their neighborhood when they spotted Norah half a block away. She sashayed down the street toward them in her purple coat. Like the Queen of England about town, my grandmother had her nose so far up in the air that she passed by my mom and aunts without seeing them. (My mother still laughs when she tells us this story.) Despite her eccentricities, Norah knew her value. She wasn't just sure of herself and the many talents she had, she believed in herself. Bacheloristas, I'm not advocating parading around with your nose up in the air (as comical as that would be), but healthy self-esteem is an absolute must.

To receive all the juicy stuff single life offers, we first need to feel worthy. Once we've got that down, let's open our hands and support each other as we tell the world much happier stories. You know, the fun ones, where we broke free of all the nonsense and began living life to its fullest. Start now, Bachelorista. The world is waiting.

THE LIFE AND LUCK OF A BACHELORISTA

"Our deepest fear is not that we are inadequate. Our deepest fear is that we are powerful beyond measure. It is our light, not our darkness that most frightens us."

– Marianne Williamson

Thank you Pippi for spiritually guiding this book.

JOIN OUR MUTUAL LOVE SOCIETY

Become part of the Bachelorista community by visiting us at www.Bachelorista.com. You'll find opportunities to share your experiences, participate in our three-day Pow-Wow, and learn more about the charities we support through our Giving Tree.

Author

After completing *The Life & Luck of a Bachelorista*, Monica Bossinger founded Bachelorista Inc. She believes that all women can blaze through their single years like a rock star, but none of us get there by going it alone.

Serving women from New York to Tokyo, Bachelorista supports and celebrates an authentic expression of single life. Ms. Bossinger lives in The Berkshires.

Illustrator

Isabelle Fregevu-Claracq is not only the Illustrator of *The Life & Luck of a Bachelorista*, but she's also the Creative Director for the brand. Using her favorite medium, watercolor, she brings the Bachelorista vision to life every day.

Isabelle lives in the South of France with her husband and son.

NOTES

NOTES

NOTES

NOTES

Made in the USA
Lexington, KY
23 May 2013